AUSTRALIAN
ABORIGINAL RELIGION

FASCICLE FOUR

INSTITUTE OF RELIGIOUS ICONOGRAPHY
STATE UNIVERSITY GRONINGEN

ICONOGRAPHY OF RELIGIONS

EDITED BY

TH. P. VAN BAAREN, L. LEERTOUWER and H. BUNING (*Secretary*)

SECTION V: AUSTRALIAN ABORIGINAL RELIGION

FASCICLE FOUR

LEIDEN
E. J. BRILL
1974

AUSTRALIAN
ABORIGINAL RELIGION

BY

RONALD M. BERNDT

FASCICLE FOUR
CENTRAL AUSTRALIA; CONCLUSION

With 39 Plates and one folding Map

LEIDEN
E. J. BRILL
1974

This Section consists of four Fascicles

ISBN 90 04 03728 4

CONTENTS

PREFACE

Fascicle Four concludes this study of Australian Aboriginal religion.

The preceding three Fascicles have looked at Aboriginal religion generally, at its basic concepts and the patterning of its various themes, recognizing that variations are just as significant to an overall understanding of religious phenomena as are more broadly based generalizations. Nevertheless, the latter are quite distinctive to Aboriginal Australia and are significant in the systematic study of comparative religions. The materials over which we have ranged have been spatially wide, extending through south-eastern and north-eastern as well as North Australia. In fact, so far, we have virtually covered three-quarters of the Australian continent. Or, to put it another way, it is probable that we have already accounted for 300 to 350 of the larger social entities that were present in Australia just before first European settlement. Of course, we have not been able to provide a total coverage: we know too little about many of these 'tribes' or language units, and too many have become extinct without our learning anything at all about them—or, at most, simply the bare outline of a few socio-cultural facts. Also, this particular study has been introductory, and it has not been possible to explore Aboriginal religion analytically except in a summarized fashion. Large cultural areas have been subsumed under more general outlines and some of the smaller areas have had to be omitted entirely. However, the broader patterning should hold good, and local variations should (from what we know about them) go to support the themes indicated here.

In our discussion of North Australia, which commenced in Fascicle Two and was completed in Fascicle Three, we were dealing with 'live' situations where traditional Aboriginal life is still in many respects an on-going reality. In the present Fascicle, the focus is again on living societies and cultures. The region covered is very wide indeed: it encompasses the central part of the Australian continent, which has been loosely termed 'Desert'—that is, relatively arid country in contrast to many other areas, notably around the coasts and permanent rivers. I have retained this convention, dividing the area conceptually into two prongs, the western and the eastern. The reasons for doing so are noted in the main text. However, on the west, in spite of the northern influences which have been filtered through the southern Kimberleys, the culture is rather more homogeneous, and so is the language— although there is considerable dialectal variation. The eastern Desert prong—with the Walbiri buffer tending to absorb and transmute northern influences—is marked by the dominating presence of the Aranda and immediately adjacent tribal groups. Throughout the Desert, including both the western and eastern prongs, the impact of the outside world has been very uneven indeed. The Aranda and adjacent groups were subjected to intensive contact at an early date, with the establishment of the Alice Springs township nearby, a mission, and pastoral stations encroaching on their tribal lands. Even though socio-cultural alterations have been considerable in their case, Professor T. G. H. Strehlow has been able to continue his work on traditional material right up to the present time. But religious belief and ritual are not 'live' in the same sense as they are in some other parts of the Desert.

The approach to this region, in this Fascicle, is the same as for the North: the focus is on the life cycle and its religious significance, on birth, initiation and death and on the mythic-inspired rituals. It was this area of Aboriginal Australia, within the eastern Desert prong, which became prominent in so much of the writing on Aboriginal religion. Through the work of Pastor Carl Strehlow and Sir Baldwin Spencer and F. J. Gillen, the world first came to know something of the intricate beliefs and rituals of the Australian Aborigines, as coherent and living systems and not as retrospective accounts. Too often, however, these were taken to apply to the whole of Aboriginal Australia, as the work of Durkheim demonstrates—despite evidence to the contrary, presented earlier by E. M. Curr, Brough Smyth and A. W. Howitt, among others. Nevertheless, the sheer quantity and quality of this material was unique for the period in which it was obtained (in the early part of this century, as far as C. Strehlow, Spencer and Gillen were concerned), and its effects on anthropological thinking have been correspondingly significant.

The final Chapter (Six) of this Fascicle is the concluding one. It spells out the major patterns of Aboriginal religious experience, and provides a general view of the meaning of Aboriginal religion.

As in other Fascicles, the bibliography is appended to the regional part—in this case, Chapter Five on Central Australia: and an additional section on iconography is included.

Department of Anthropology,   Ronald M. BERNDT
University of Western Australia

CHAPTER FIVE

CENTRAL AUSTRALIA

This region is bounded on the north, as we have seen, by the Walbiri—a tribe which, in spite of its northern influences, is basically of Desert orientation. The Walmadjeri, who now live at Balgo and other places in the southern Kimberleys and on the northwest coast of Western Australia, and the Gugadja-Mandjildjara who moved out of the Desert in roughly the same directions, also face toward the Desert—or, so to speak, look backward at it over their shoulders. Both the Walbiri and the Gugadja-Mandjildjara, especially, are of the Desert and belong to Central traditions: they influence each other; and each has further associations which stretch out into different areas of the Desert.

These socio-cultural linkages spell greater involvement with, and within, a linguistic-cultural bloc which is the largest in Aboriginal Australia, possessing a common culture with variations, and a common language with differing dialects. This is usually called the Western Desert bloc. Its western prong covers an immense area falling within three states, in Western, South and Central Australia (see R. Berndt 1959: 81-107). It extends south-ward from the Balgo area to Laverton and then eastward, north of the transcontinental railtrack, including the central core of ranges—the Warburtons in the west and the Ever-ards in the east. The eastern prong, stretching south from the Walbiri in the Northern Territory, is part of the same Western Desert culture, but in this case there is a more direct link with the Aranda of Central Australia, and it is less homogeneous. For example, the Aranda, as they are generally labelled, stand out in contrast to the Western Desert Bidjandjara- (or Pitjantjatara- Aluridja-) speaking people, in cultural and linguistic terms. This division is a useful one for purposes of discussion, although there is considerable overlap between the two broad areas we shall be examining.

A. THE LIFE CYCLE: THE WESTERN PRONG

1. *Birth*

(Unless specifically stated otherwise, the material in this section is derived from R. and C. Berndt 1942-45, supplemented by unpublished field notes.)

Western Desert Aborigines were not ignorant of physiological paternity and maternity, even though their knowledge was not scientifically exact. However, the physical aspects were submerged by the belief in spiritual association. In this belief, the nucleus of spirit-animators was to be found at particular *julan'gabi* (yulan gabi) (spirit-centre waterholes). These spirits came into existence mostly through the actions of various mythical characters, particularly Minma Waiuda (Possum Woman) and Minma Milbali (White Goanna Woman). Children who are potentially linked by various totems when born may all come from one *julan'gabi*. The spirits bring with them some of the life-essence inherent in the Dreaming (*djugur*), and are consequently sacred themselves. The emphasis is on the actual place of birth. Ideally, this should be in the local group territory of the child's father. A child so born inherits his father's mythic associations, which are those of that territory and of a specific waterhole or constellation of waterholes within it (see R. Berndt 1959: 97-101). Through a movement away from such territories to the fringe settlements as a direct and indirect result of alien contact, there has been a weakening of ties with particular local sites —but not with the cult totem tracks, which are patrilineally defined. Increasingly, birth along such a track is taken to be sufficient to endorse ties with a father's local group.

The assumption is that a particular manifestation of a Dreaming or mythic being enters a pregnant woman and takes up residence in the foetus, which is simultaneously animated by the spirit child, thus providing it with human life. Prior to that, the foetus simply grows as part of the mother. The animator gives it a life of its own, as well as making mythic identification possible. Beliefs concerning this transformation vary, and are often vague; but one suggestion is that birth could not take place, even though the foetus had been animated, without the spiritual presence of a mythic being.

Mountford (1948: 158-60) too speaks of *yulanya* (spirit children) at Ernabella who await an opportunity to enter pregnant women: they are themselves of the Dreaming. In the north-western part of the Desert, the *djugur* (cult lodge or local descent group totem) is sometimes separated from, sometimes identified with, the *djarin* (conception totem), as in the Balgo area. At Jigalong (near Lake Disappointment), the conception totem is *djarinba*, and a person's 'cult' totem depends usually upon his place of 'conception' or birth (Tonkinson 1966: 209-11). The concept of *djarin* is a northern tradition: while the *julan'gordi* (*julan* spirit) is much more typical of the Desert and ensures a double linkage, as it were, with the sacred.

2. *Initiation*

The initiation of Gugadja-Mandjildjara and Walmadjeri novices can be seen as a bridge between northern, eastern and southern traditions. Southern Desert initiation includes the instruction of novices, who are guided through rituals that are gradually revealed to them. Again, as we saw in Chapter Four, it is relatively easy to separate out initiation *per se*, as having a distinctive ritual content and intent: but many of the rites included in later stages are revelatory. For the Balgo-Jigalong regions, after the preliminaries, a novice is removed from the main camp and is regarded as ritually 'dead': he is circumcised, and receives his first bullroarer. Then he is anointed with blood, which he also drinks, and ritual re-enactments of mythical events are revealed and explained.

In the south-western and eastern Desert areas, initiation is more highly formalized. It is substantiated by a number of initiatory myths: for example, by the myths of the Wadi Gudara (the Two Men), Malu (Kangaroo), Kanjala (Euro) and Djurdju (a Night Bird), among others, in the Ooldea area; and by Malu and Wadi Baba (Dog Man) in the Laverton-Warburton area. (See R. and C. Berndt 1964/68: 206-8.) These myths outline what should be done in such circumstances, and often provide reasons. One interesting mythological point concerns circumcision. Originally it was done with a firestick, burning off the foreskin. However, this resulted, so the myth reports, in the death of novices, and a stone flake was introduced by Kalaia (Emu) women. Also, simultaneously with male initiation, female novices were deflowered: but hymen-cutting was later substituted. Traditionally, male and female initiation rites were held at the same time, and the relevant mythology even adds that the same stone flakes should be used. In the great Njirana-Julana (Yulana) myth cycle, these two Dreaming men (as 'father' and 'son', or as man and his own penis) were circumcised by the Minmara group of women (see below). Myths state clearly that women were initially responsible for circumcising male novices, and in this respect there is some similarity with more northern versions.

The choice of the actual series of mythic re-enactments at such a time depends on a novice's own local descent group or cult lodge. For example, if he belongs to the Wadi Gudara, then all the songs and ritual sequences that are performed for him refer to these mythic beings. If he is a Malu youth, he is shown the Wadi Malu cycle; and so on. However, this does not preclude sections of other cycles being sung or performed. Some of these have a fairly wide currency in the context of initiation, and a lot depends on the extent of territory covered by a particular mythic being—that is, his track. Nevertheless, given this variation in content, the sequential structure of initiation remains more or less constant.

Traditionally, the first stage involves wailing for novices, who are regarded as passing into a ritual state of death. The first rite consists of obtaining blood from the arm veins of initiated men. This is collected in a wooden dish, and is passed round so that all, including novices, sip from it. Novices then have blood smeared over their bodies. Blood has a two-fold symbolic significance. It emphasizes a novice's ritual death while at the same time providing him with life: and it unites all participants in a common commitment. The first stage includes piercing of the nasal septum, and tooth evulsion, which are not ritually significant: like cicatrization, they have probably come into the Desert from the east. Partial segregation is traditionally maintained for a lengthy period, continuing while a novice moves with his group across the country; but under present-day conditions it is considerably telescoped. The second stage ushers in the more important preliminary ritual. For instance, a novice is conventionally beaten by his immediate male and female relatives. Then he is ritually tossed, a rite which has mythological significance but is generally said to represent the termination of his seclusion period, when he is given a pearlshell necklet and waistband.

This is followed by a fire-throwing rite near the circumcision ground, when women perform a shuffling dance with feet apart, making deep grooves in the sand. Mythologically, this is a re-enactment of the actions of the Minmara or Gunggaranggara women in the Njirana-Julana cycle. (See R. and C. Berndt 1964/68: 208-9 for one version.) In the actual initiation sequence, as the women reach the fires which have been placed near the ground, men throw firebrands at and over them and they retreat. This ritual act is also mentioned by Mountford (1938: 252) and Tindale (1935: 212-3). It represents antagonism between generation levels— between women of the novice's generation (who dance) and those of his parents and classificatory children's level.

These events are followed by several mythic dramatic performances, mainly involving men of the novices' own patrilineal local descent groups or mythic tracks. After that, the novices are smoked. Dancing men hold bunches of green boughs, in which lighted tinder has been placed, to produce billowing smoke which is said to counteract dangerous influences. Then, a human circumcision-table is formed and novices are carried one by one along a pathway made by the smoke-dancers, and arranged on the men's backs for cutting. After the operation, they are guided back to their own camp and remain there until their wounds are healed. At this time, novices are given two bullroarers, and their hair is bound in the 'bun' style of a newly-initiated man. Blood is spurted over them again, and they are brought back to the main camp, 'sung in' by men and women. Traditionally, following these rites, youths were taken on a pilgrimage to sacred sites within their own local descent group territory or along the track of their own cult totem (cult myth), retracing the actions of that being.

Tindale's (1935: 199-224) description of initiation, up to the concluding rites of circumcision, is a variation on this theme. Gould's general account (1969:104-20) puts subincision into the primarily circumcisional sequence. However, in his account the various stages follow in different order, and firebrand throwing is not accompanied by the distinctive groove-dancing of the women: nor is this followed by tossing.

Post-circumcisional rites in the Desert focus mainly on the revelation of sacred mythic re-enactments and the use of various objects. Subincision takes place one or two years after circumcision, and at some distance from the main camp: it is only after this that a man may marry. There is a great deal of mythic information on this rite. Although it is the most sacred of all ritual, it is initially, when the first incision is made, quite informal. Its significance lies principally in the act of subincising itself, and the rites that follow this: see R. and C. Berndt 1945: 239-66 and R. Berndt 1965: 187-9. (In the framework we are discussing, subincision is connected with the northern tradition.) However, after subincision, there is a period of segregation during which men spurt blood from their penis incisures over the novices; this is accompanied by dancing and singing, mainly connected with the Wadi Gudara and Njirana-Julana cycles. It has been suggested by several writers that the purpose of subincision is to replicate female menstruation. In regions farther north where the *kunapipi* (in one form or another) is a basic part of religious life, this association is explicitly stated: post-subincisional dancing in this context involves blood-letting from the penis at regular intervals—similar, it is said, to the menstrual flow. In such dancing, the blood splashes over the men's thighs. In the Desert, subincision may be carried out for therapeutic reasons, and this view is supported by myth.

It is only after subincision that an initiate becomes actively engaged in secret-sacred life. Regular ritual incisure-piercing accompanies the re-enactment of major dramatic sequences. However, once his post-subincisional seclusion period is over, the youth is taken to a dancing ground where the women are covered with branches (or blankets). A feast is held, and when the women have left, the initiate is shown the long sacred wooden boards (the *tjilbilba*) for the first time. This feast gains in importance in the north-western sector of the Desert (and its extension), where it is called the *mididi* or *midajidi*. Petri (1960) notes that (at Anna Plains and at La Grange) it takes place after circumcision; Tonkinson (1966) says it is held (in the Jigalong area) about two years after subincision, and it is then that the symbolism of the sacred boards is explained to the new initiates.

In the Desert, cicatrization is regarded as a final rite. It is of the (non-Desert) eastern tradition, and is carried out publicly without accompanying songs or dancing.

In summary, then, initiation in the Desert has distinctive features which are influenced by various traditions. There is a much greater emphasis on a novice's ritual death and revival through being anointed with blood, than through the medium of a mythic being's womb (for example, via the Mother). Except in the north-west of the Desert, the sacred ground does not symbolize a womb through which novices and postulants pass in order to be reborn. In all areas, north and south, mythic substantiation involves more than one ancestral or spirit being. In the north, in contrast to the Desert, there is the integrating influence of a major being like the Fertility Mother. In the Desert, the ritual of initiation, in spite of its general patterning, relies more heavily on specific Dreaming tracks. Religious ideology is much more coordinated in the north than in the Desert. In the Desert it is much more segmentary, and the reasons for this are to be found in the social structure.

An emphasis on ritual death is clear, too, in the Desert initiation of girls at puberty, when—traditionally—the hymen is cut. The seclusion period that follows is explicitly regarded as being a ritual death; it is only after a girl has been painted and decorated and has a pearlshell of lifegiving properties hung from her neck that she is restored to normal life. There is disparity between males and females in the preparation for adulthood. The focus for girls is on physical maturity, which comes earlier than for boys. A major consideration, for boys, is the need to prepare them for their ideal role as repositories of traditional religious knowledge. For them, socialization into adult life is concurrently, and almost by definition, socialization into religious affairs: and it means, inescapably, increasing involvement in sacred matters. In the Desert, the initiatory period not only commences later than it does farther north; it also involves a more extensive range of physical trials.

3. *Death*

Throughout the Desert, the disposal of a corpse is by burial. However, the grave is not filled in but is covered with leaves, boughs and logs. A conical mound is constructed at one end, and into this is stuck a digging stick for a woman, a spear for a man. The mound is associated with Wadi Bira (Moon Man), who was 'killed' by the Wadi Gudara. Moon is almost inevitably cast for this role, and his death and revival are treated generally in Aboriginal mythology. In the Desert, Wadi Bira (or Gidjili) attempted to seduce one of the Wadi Gudara's wives. For this he was later castrated by the Two Men and his penis metamorphosed as stone. He also fought the Wadi Keniga (Native Cat Man): but when he was killed, he always revived, and a reminder of this is the grave-side mound: this implies the potential rebirth of the deceased person. However, the pattern of disposal is of the delayed variety. Some months elapse before the mortuary party returns to make observations, for divinatory purposes, and then to remove the bones and to rub the sand which has adhered to them, or the decomposing flesh or fluids if these are still there, over their own legs or bodies. (See Berndt and Johnston 1942.)

The deceased's spirit (*gordi*), which entered his body before birth, leaves it with his last breath, but does not return immediately to its *julan* spirit child centre. Part of it remains in a special *njunjunba* mourning ring, which is made by a sibling of the deceased and retained by the widow, or widower. Another part remains near the corpse, even after burial. Mourners speak to it, and then drive it into the grave. But during the period from initial burial until the bones are re-interred, it is believed to wander far afield and associate with malignant *mamu* spirits as well as with Wonambi, the great water-snake or Rainbow Snake. On the return of the burial party, the spirit is summoned by the widow or widower and a native doctor, and is attracted to the grave by a smoking fire. The native doctor catches it (or part of it), places it in his stomach, and uses it as a special spirit agent in divination. Later he releases it, and it returns to its *julan'gabi* (spirit waterhole). The *njunjunba* is eventually thrown into a waterhole associated with Wonambi, who is said to swallow it.

In marked contrast to other Aboriginal areas, these people recognize no specific Land of the Dead. The Moon myth reflects the belief that human beings are caught in an inescapable cycle marked by periodic transition, of changing status, with the expectation that one always returns because one is of the Dreaming. It is not necessary to die to achieve immortality: immortality is a condition of man. This is a fundamental tenet of Desert religious belief.

A comparison is drawn, in R. and C. Berndt (1964/68: 183, figs. 11 and 12), between the life cycles of north-eastern Arnhem Land and the Great Victoria Desert respectively. While it is clear that in the Desert there is a direct linkage between the deceased person's spirit and the *djugur* (Dreaming), it is a relationship which is paralleled by the sequence that is inherent in the *julan* spirit itself. Both belong to the Dreaming, and both (as one) have the expectation of being reborn in human form, bringing with them, into the world of man, the essence of sacredness. Nevertheless, the framework of belief is not necessarily as straightforward as this. Intervening elements, for example the *mamu*, reveal ambiguities. The presence of Wonambi offers a key of some importance. In the north the Rainbow, as the Great Snake, is almost always directly associated with general fertility, with rain and with spirit children. In the Desert, Wonambi is the guardian of native doctors, as he is in the northern fringe areas of Balgo and Birrundudu. (See R. and C. Berndt 1950: 185, plate 3. Mountford 1948: 133-40, too, provides some comments.) Wonambi presides at the initiation of native doctors: he swallows initiands and then vomits them. In all cases, Wonambi has the power to revivify, and it is probably for this reason that he appears in association with the deceased's spirit.

B. Religious Rituals: the Western Prong

In the north-western Desert, southward to Jigalong, the coordinating structures of the *gurangara* and *dingari* have produced a degree of overall formalization which was less evident in the traditional Desert religion. An example of initiation has already been mentioned, where the structure, in the shape of its sequential stages, is apparently recognized by all Desert Aborigines. Certain actions must be carried out in all cases, and their symbolism is more or less agreed upon. The differences lie in the actual content of the songs and the associated mythic representations which are revealed to novices: and these are dependent primarily on the local group sponsoring the initiation. Such actions are not, of course, separated from their total cycles. At any one initiation sequence, representatives of several local groups will be present: and they have their part to play in the ritual. Additionally, as noted, some myths are more directly relevant to initiation (for example, circumcision and subincision). Nevertheless, the focus of religious life is on particular *djugur* Dreaming lines or tracks, the paths taken by specific spirit beings in their travels across the countryside. Some of these are very extensive indeed.

Essentially, it is the local descent group, its numbers relatively small, which possesses a stretch of country associated with one or more *djugur(ba)* male or female spirit beings. Its members, especially its male members, have the responsibility of watching over this section of the myth and songs, and its ritual expression. However, such mythic tracks extend much farther than does the territory of a local descent group; only rarely do they correspond exactly. Ordinarily the tracks continue across the country, so that any one of them is shared among several local descent groups—which in totality constitute a 'religious group', or a 'cult lodge', as it has been called by Elkin (1934: 171-92). These paths are vitally significant, and Elkin (*ibid.*) emphasizes the need for a child to be born on a path associated with his father's local country.

Each mythic path, then, serves as a focus for religious activity: it is complete within itself. It is true that, at the mythic level, some of these paths intersect: particular mythic characters form marital and food-collecting units so that spirit beings belonging to other paths are often present: there is a tendency toward an interlocking of mythic perspective. Nevertheless, all mythic ritual is relevant to tracks or paths expressed in song and action, even though people connected with other tracks are present. Because some of the myth-paths are so extensive, it would be impossible to dramatize the whole sequence at any one time without drastically altering the whole style of ritual organization. Mythic knowledge is therefore fragmented in respect of any one path. It is also fragmented in respect of the total mythic tradition of the people. The total religion of these Desert Aborigines is, as it were, held in a series of parcels which are distributed among many local groups.

This religious perspective is in marked contrast to religious organization farther north, where there are coordinating structures, and even in the north-west of the Desert itself where, for example, the *dingari* has similar over-arching ramifications. The reasons rest, firstly, on the fact that we are considering a relatively large socio-cultural bloc. Secondly, it probably has to do with the greater mobility of the Desert people, and perhaps the larger territorial spread of group movements—greater than in northern areas. However, all local Desert groups, and their mythic paths, do hold in common certain symbolic representations or ritual objects. These are mainly sacred boards or flat slabs of wood bearing incised designs that relate to the travels and adventures of the mythic beings. They also represent the bodies of these beings, and are treated as such.

The cult lodges are responsible for rites centred on these sacred boards and particular relics, for post-subincision blood-letting rites, and for dramatic re-enactments of mythical events. They are also involved in rites to maintain the supply of natural species, either held at specific 'increase' sites or included indirectly in more comprehensive dramatic sequences. In the southern and south-western Desert, as far north as the Warburtons, some rites are focused on particular secret-sacred relics. For example, two stones are the metamorphosed bodies of the Two Men, the Wadi Gudara, one representing the body of Kulgabi or Milbali (White Goanna), the other the body of Jungga (Yungga; Black Goanna). Others are the *tjilbilba* board associated with the Wadi Gudara and taken into the sky by the Dreaming Child, Wudulu, to become the Milky Way; the stone eggs of Jungga and Milbali women; the stone shield of the Wadi Gudara; a stone dish representing a Milbali woman. Another relic is a desiccated human body, said to be a Milbali woman. Such relics move along their mythic tracks and across the Desert, and are connected with meditation as well as with blood-letting. The Wadi Gudara relics are the subject of special rites. Local descent group headmen carrying them howl ritually—like the howling in the mythic period which signified the giving of the religious law to the Desert people, before the Two Men took on the appearance of goanna; and as they howl, they drive the women and young men before them, from one waterhole to the next—travelling as did the mythic beings themselves.

Within the confines of this study, it is not possible to detail the myths and ritual actions of all or any one local descent group or mythic path. The mythic beings are essentially shape-changing—sometimes human in form, sometimes in the form of a natural species. They are eternal; their power can be brought to bear on contemporary events. Further, they are manifested through their living counterparts, those who now perform the appropriate ritual by virtue of their spiritual association, which is derived through having been born on the path or in the local territory of a particular mythic being.

Blood-letting rites are carried out by virtually all cult lodges. The simplest of these involve anointing the bodies of novices and postulants; anointing specific increase centres (to provide material life for the mythic spirit of a particular natural species associated with that site or sites); and using blood as an adhesive for decorating postulants who perform mythic ritual acts. There is also the drinking of blood—for example, from the Waiuda (Possum woman) wooden dish. In the substantiating myth, Minma Waiuda is sent by her husband, Djurdju (Night Bird; a small White Night Owl), to be initiated by the Two Men. Later he sends her to them again, this time for a magical *maban* shell. However, an avoidance tabu now exists between her and the Two Men, because they initiated her. She therefore avoids them and goes toward the west, where she turns into an opossum. Her husband follows her and burns the tree in which she has taken refuge. She then turns into the Waiuda dish. In memory of her, the Two Men dig a pit, spurt arm blood into the dish which they have placed alongside it, then mix a little sand with the blood. Each in turn lies in the pit while the other rubs the blood and sand into his hair; this symbolizes Waiuda's death, and the rubbing of blood and sand into their hair her, and their, revivification. In the contemporary rite, too, men dig a pit on the sacred ground and place the dish beside it: wailing continues in the main camp; and later, when the fully initiated men return to the sacred ground, they howl. Two men of the Wadi Gudara local descent group spurt blood from their arm veins into the pit, and a little of this is given to each of those present. It is said to be the 'actual blood' of the spirit beings.

In the ritual performances put on by the cult lodges, various headdresses and appendages are worn and used: for example, the long wooden *tjilbilba* boards, the *laralara* (or extended *wanigi* or thread-cross), the ordinary smaller *wanigi*, and the bullroarer. The decorations are of great variety, and there are special sets for each mythic being. All of the rites are accompanied by songs, arranged in cycles. Among the people who came south to the Ooldea area in the early 1940's, for instance, the major cult rituals centred on the wanderings of the Two Men; Njirana and Julana (and the Minmara or Gunggaranggara women); Mingari (Mountain Devil woman) and Baba (Dog); Malu (Kangaroo), Kanjala (Euro) and Djurdju (Night Bird, or Owl); Malu and Baba (from the northern sector of the Desert); Gulber (Blue Kangaroo) and Keniga (Native Cat); Waiuda (Possum woman), and so on. Several versions of these are given by R. and C. Berndt (1942-45; 1964/68: 205-9, 223-4, 227, 228), Mountford (1937: 5-28) and Tindale (1936: 169-85; 1959: 305-32). While some names remain constant over large areas of the Desert, others may vary from one local region to another.

Although, as mentioned, many of these rites re-enact the travels of such beings, many are also, at the same time, focused on everyday affairs. In fact, the myths and their ritual counterparts can be viewed as statements about Desert living. In the Western Desert, 'the physical, social and cultural environments of mythic man virtually coincide with those relevant to traditional and present-day non-acculturated Aboriginal man ...' (Berndt 1970: 243-4). Certainly, these myths deal with basic issues of social living. They treat in symbolic terms the relations between men and women, between sacred and mundane, and between materialistic and spiritual or transcendental issues. All of them imply 'a pre-occupation with the vicissitudes of Desert living, an endeavour to cope with an essentially unpredictable environment, by making it ritually predictable'. The mythic characters, once their magical qualities are discounted, resemble very closely indeed ordinary human characters, as do their actions in traditional terms. The myths and rituals of these Aborigines reflect their own vital concerns, as one would expect them to do.

In contrast to the southern Desert, the people who have come into Jigalong from the Desert farther to the east (Tonkinson 1970: 277-91; Mountford and Tonkinson 1969: 371-90) draw a distinction between ritual directly derived from the creative era, which they term *mangundjanu*, and *badundjaridjanu*, which is ritual derived through the dream-spirit journeys of local Aboriginal men. We can call the first vertically defined, in contrast to horizontally defined ritual. The first corresponds to the normal ritual *djugur* pattern already discussed. The second involves elders or native doctors who, during sleep and in the form of dream-spirits, are believed to travel on a length of hair-string or ride astride a long sacred board to a far distant waterhole. There, for example, spirit children show them dances and songs performed and sung by spirit creatures in totemic form. It is on the basis of such experiences that new rituals come into being. Examples of this kind are much more common in the north-central area (Wave Hill, and the eastern and southern Kimberleys) than in the Desert proper. The riding of sacred boards has its parallel in the Balgo area among people closely related to those now settled at Jigalong, in the exploits of mythic beings (R. Berndt 1970: 224-32), and at Birrundudu in the travels of native doctors when they ride astride a Rainbow Snake (R. and C. Berndt 1950: plate 3).

Over and above dramatic performances, ritual activity aimed at the maintenance of natural species is not in the northern pattern of generalized fertility, but is compartmentalized. Members of specific local descent groups are responsible for attending to particular increase sites. Such sites are linked with the mythic beings and are a part of major myth cycles. Additionally, there are magico-religious rites for rain and for love magic, and these are also well within the orbit of mythic sponsorship. Mythic beings are responsible too for sorcery or destructive forms of magic; the power which is believed to make such acts efficacious comes from them. Any broader study of Aboriginal religious phenomena would need to take these aspects into account. For instance, in the Desert area (as noted) the initiation of native doctors is directly linked with Wonambi, and the ritual is said to include the swallowing and vomiting-out of postulants. There is a close similarity here to ordinary northern initiation ritual, as far as symbolism is concerned.

One aspect which does not receive the attention one would expect in a relatively arid area is rain-making. Of course, there are magical rites connected with it, but they are mostly of a minor nature. Rain can be made, it is said, by any person simply scraping a pearlshell ('water-bearing' shells); by a native doctor undoing a rain bundle secreted in his beard; or by a collective rite performed by men wearing special decorations, and head-dresses resembling snakes, said to be representations of Wonambi, who is nearly always associated with water. One explanation for the paucity of rain-making rites, in contrast to so many others, is that there is nearly always water to be had in one way or another—through permanent waters, soaks, water-bearing plants, roots, etc. Another is that these Aborigines are used to their natural environment and take it very much for granted. However, these attitudes are not uniform throughout the Desert, and among people now living in the Jigalong area (Tonkinson 1966) rain-making rites are much more formalized and elaborate. Some of these are secret-sacred, and relate to a Dreaming character named Djaramara. The songs describe different types of clouds, rain and lightning. In a number of these, men, women and children participate together. (Tonkinson 1970: 285-7.)

In the southern Desert, women's religious life is of major importance, as it is elsewhere. Here, female characters are just as frequent in the Dreaming as males are. There is also a repertoire of myths known and told by women. Women have a significant part to play in regard to the secret-sacred rites of men, and have their own secret rituals focused on Dreaming objects, representing (e.g.) a Black Goanna. They also have a large selection of love magic—for example, the Carpet Snake rite. The wider implications of these have been discussed by C. Berndt (1965: 238-82).

C. The Life Cycle: the Eastern Prong

1. *Birth*

A linkage with the sacred, as far as the pre-natal spirit is concerned, commences (for the eastern prong) with the Walbiri (see Chapter Four) and southern Kimberleys examples. In both these cases the connection is clear. What differences there are, lie in the degree of identification between the spirit child and a specific Dreaming character. Although both are of the Dreaming, and by definition sacred, spirit children are more free-ranging and may serve as intermediaries between pregnant women and particular sites (associated with specific beings) at which such women either realize they have conceived (i.e., the 'conception' site) or give birth to a child. In the southern Kimberleys, the 'conception' spirit may be identified with the mythic indicator, referring to the local descent group of the pregnant woman's husband. The south-western prong of the Desert brings together the diffuse spirit-child belief and the local descent group Dreaming with its patrilineal emphasis.

Munn (1970: 146), for the northern Bidjandjara (at Areyonga), underlines a person's close associations with his birthplace and its ancestors, identifying himself with them and demonstrating that identification by a birthmark (*djuguridja*, 'of or pertaining to the ancestors'—the Dreaming). This is said to have been left at his birthplace by the ancestor. Speaking for the southern Walbiri at Yuendumu, Munn (*ibid.*: 148) notes that 'A person is thought to have the ancestral powers [*guruwari*: compare with Meggitt, 1962] of that ancestor inside him, and these powers are also thought to have entered his or her mother at that place' (where he or she has been conceived). And this is in addition to ancestral affiliations determined by patrilineal descent.

In the Aranda situation (Strehlow 1947: 86-96), the spiritual entry to its human vehicle is at 'conception' (quickening; awareness of pregnancy), so that a person's ownership of sacred *tjurunga* is decided by his 'conception site'. On recognizing conception, a woman 'tells her husband of her experience and shows him the exact spot where she first became aware of her condition' (*ibid.*: 87). He consults with others, and they decide which ancestor caused the woman's pregnancy. The mythic being is said to have either entered her body himself or hurled a small bullroarer at her hips. 'The child when born will belong to the totem of this ancestor'. This is the western Aranda belief. For the northern Aranda it is similar, but 'conception' there can be attributed to the eating of vegetable food—however, only those foods associated with a particular totem being (*ibid.*: 90). Among the southern Aranda, *tjurunga* are stored in small bundles 'at the exact sites where the ancestors lived and wandered about ...' A woman approaching one of these sites may hear a cry which she thinks is a child crying, and feel unwell: an ancestor has entered her. Or she may actually 'see' a child, which enters her. Generally, in the Aranda area, the actual birthplace of a child is of no significance. In this respect, it is the ancestor who has been reincarnated in human form. Soon after the birth of a child, his *tjurunga* are determined—through the mythic actions of the ancestor who caused his conception. Strehlow (1970: 97) says that children 'tended to have their conception sites ... located in the group areas of the parents'.

Strehlow also notes (1965: 127) that it is a 'personal emotional link uniting every individual with his birthplace [in the Western Desert] or his conception site [in the Aranda-speaking area], also with the main totemic centre of his patrilineal group, that distinguished Aboriginal religion'.

In the earlier literature, Spencer and Gillen (1938: 112-6) give a number of examples of this kind for areas outside the Aranda territories as well as within them. They state (*ibid.*: 124) that a woman 'conceives' a child near a particular site: it is the spirit of that site which enters her, and this is irrespective of what her or her husband's totem may be. This substantiates Strehlow's point—except that, as he remarks, there is a tendency for a child's totem to be associated with the local descent group of a parent. Spencer and Gillen (*ibid.*: 336-8) report a myth in which a Dreaming boy went into the ground taking with him a store of *tjurunga*, and from this a stone arose (the *erathipa*); this is the centre of a plum tree totem, the stone being the home of many spirits, each associated with a *tjurunga*. At one side of this stone is a hole, through which spirit children leave to enter women. Over the hole a black line is painted, and renewed from time to time; a similar line is painted above the eyes of a newly-born child, and is believed to prevent sickness. Other *erathipa* (child) stones are found at different sites. (See also Spencer and Gillen 1904: 145 *et seq.*)

2. *Initiation*

Walbiri and northern Desert (southern Kimberley influenced) forms of initiation have been discussed. The western variation on this theme closely approximates the northern Bidjandjara and more north-easterly Desert people in the Yuendumu area. Munn (1970: 153) speaks of initiation at Yuendumu (Walbiri) as being close to Meggitt's (1962) example, in which the thread-cross is used (among other things) and placed on a novice's chest. This enables the lodge (local descent group) patrispirit to enter him: 'the powers of the object are imprinted in the novice'. She emphasizes that initiation is 'a kind of dying', and 'the novice is then "reborn" into a world where he may begin to participate in ceremonials involving the re-creation and control of ancestral transformations'.

Spencer and Gillen (1938: 212-70) give a detailed description of Aranda initiation, which they divide into five stages: painting and tossing of novices; actual circumcision; head biting; subincision; and fire ritual (the *engwura*). Between the tossing and circumcision several years may elapse. The *engwura* (*ibid.*: 270-386), include a large range of rites which more properly fall under the general title of revelatory ritual—although, of course, all involve the acceptance of novices and postulants. Basedow (1925: 230-56) also has a brief sketch of Aluridja (Western Desert; Bidjandjara) and Aranda initiation ritual.

Strehlow (1947: 97-119) says that the main initiatory rites for males are carried out on the secret-sacred *pulla* ground. A novice witnesses, before his first operation, some of the rituals of his clan, and immediately afterward receives a large bullroarer: he is then a *rukuta* and must learn the secret language which is spoken between initiated men; he also commences to learn the sacred songs of his group. His post-circumcisional period is one of learning. Following circumcision comes head biting. The scalp is opened by means of a sharp stick, and then bitten by old men so that blood flows profusely. Ostensibly, this is to promote the growth of hair. After a short period, subincision takes place; and this is regarded as being the most important of all, since it has implications for adult activity, involving regular incisure opening (see below). This is followed by the *ingkura* festival (that is, Spencer and Gillen's *engwura*), which Strehlow includes under initiation.

In the circumcisional ritual (Spencer and Gillen *ibid.*: 220-1), women first dance bearing shields. The mythic reason for this is that in the Dreaming, the Unthippa women carried, in the course of their travels, a number of young boys who had been initiated. In the present-day ritual a novice is brought through the dancing women to the *pulla* ground, and the sound of bullroarers symbolizes the spirit Twanyikara (*twanjiraka*, large bullroarer) who will carry him away. A novice is also handed a firestick. On the whole, Aranda initiation is more formalized than its southern Desert counterpart, mainly because there is a greater emphasis on instruction, and a larger number of mythic dramatic re-enactments. In the subincision rites, certain women cicatrize themselves in the main camp, while their male relatives are being subincised: and these cuts, say Spencer and Gillen (*ibid.*: 257), are often represented by line-markings on *tjurunga*. Women also assemble and dance in the main camp at this time, and there is a certain amount of ritual interaction between men and women: for example, a newly subincised man has hair cut from him; and he throws a boomerang toward his mother's Dreaming site—that is, it is said, *at* the mythic being incarnated through his mother. Spencer and Gillen (*ibid.*: 259) see this as symbolizing the subincised man's release from his mother's influence. However, all initiation ritual in this context, as in others, is a symbolic discourse between men and women in socio-physical terms: an exercise in male-female relations—circumcision representing the male aspect, subincision the female aspect.

The *ingkura* ground is, according to Strehlow (1947: 100-12), 'the real initiation centre of any group'. Here, initiated youths are instructed in the myths and songs of their own clan (local group). At the beginning of these *ingkura*, every young man (*iliara* or *maliera*: a term widely used in the southern and western Kimberleys as in Central Australia: see Meggitt, 1966: 3), receives a new *tjurunga* (known as *namatuna*, a small bullroarer) which is decorated in his own totemic patterning. These bullroarers are frequently swung, and men re-enact ritually the appropriate myths. Over a period, all the sacred *tjurunga* of a particular *ingkura* ground must be exhibited, since each *ingkura* is focused on a specific myth sequence. Sometimes these take months to perform. The *tnatantja* and *kauaua* poles are also exhibited; these stand near a sacred earthmound which is an essential part of every *ingkura*. Finally, the *kauaua* is uprooted and the *iliara* dance with it before returning to the camp. Spencer and Gillen (*ibid.*: 271-386) give descriptive details of these *ingkura*. In one section, women and children gather together on a flat stretch of ground where they prepare a fire. Youths going through the *ingkura* rites are driven toward the women, who respond by throwing lighted brands at them, while men with swinging bullroarers run round them. The men then return to the sacred earthmound. This is repeated in different contexts. Later, the fire throwing is reversed, and youths going through the *ingkura* throw firebrands across the heads of the women and children. This is followed by taking the sacred *tjurunga* to the women's camp and showing it to them. Spencer and Gillen (*ibid.*: 369) say that the reason for this exhibition lies in the Dreaming—spirit women then carried *tjurunga* about with them. However, in the *ingkura*, although the sacred *tjurunga* is taken to the women, it is hidden by the men—who fall upon it, completely covering it. A further rite is the steaming of the *ingkura* initiands, who are made to lie full length on green boughs placed over a fire.

At Macumba in north-eastern South Australia, in the early 1940's, a mixed Andingari-Aranda initiation ritual was held, involving during the same period both circumcision and subincision. (These have been described in R. and C. Berndt 1945: 239-60, Appendix 1.) The main sequence included groove-dancing by women, throwing of firesticks, and covering of a novice 'as if he were dead'. While the novice was covered, men opened their penis incisures and danced the special shuffling dance which caused blood to flow from their wounds. (Shavings smeared with penis blood were worn in a headband similar to that of the mythic being Njirana.) The subincision songs and dances then switched to songs and dances of circumcision—in front of a novice, who was told about the meanings of the mythic re-enactments. When the men returned to the main camp, with the entry of visitors, penis-holding took place (see also R. and C. Berndt 1945: 260-66; R. Berndt 1965: 189-90). Bullroarers were not used, in this context, for the pre-circumcisional rites. However, a number of dramatic performances were shown to the novices. In the final section, women danced diagonally across the flat ground in the fashion of the mythical Gunggaranggara women, toward the breakwind were the men were assembled. Firesticks were then thrown by men toward and over the heads of the women; and, in turn, by women toward and over the heads of the men. Then the novices, perched astride men's shoulders, were shown to the women from behind the windbreak. At the sight of them, the women turned and hurried back to the main camp, wailing. Afterward, novices were circumcised; and later, as they warmed their penes over a fire, they were made to get up and embrace the *wanigi* (thread-cross), rubbing their newly cut penes against it.

Spencer and Gillen (*ibid.*), it will be recalled, mention that women have a significant role to play in male initiation; Strehlow (*ibid.*) emphasizes their importance in myth; see also C. Berndt (1965: 238-82). Spencer and Gillen (*ibid.*: 93-6) refer to hymen-cutting in the south-western Desert, said to be equivalent to subincision: the operation for females being *atna-ariltha-kuma*; for males, *pura-ariltha-kuma*. Before the operation, a girl's vulva was touched with a small *tjurunga* to prevent too great a flow of blood. This rite preceded marriage, and followed first menstruation: there were also rites to promote the growth of a girl's breasts (*ibid.*: 459-60).

Initiatory patterns, then, for males and females (for females in conjunction with males, or for males separated from females within the context of the secret-sacred), with certain variations, are roughly similar throughout the Desert. Males undergo formal instruction, while female initiation serves primarily as a preparation for marriage. Men are formally the principal custodians of their 'tribal lore', and are consequently prepared for that role.

Although the intent is different for each sex, it is recognized that this is not a strict division of the sacred in sexual terms. The importance of women, mythically and ritually, in company with men, is clearly stated. One thing which initiation does underline, in terms of community effort, is participation by all of its adult members in a series of sacred acts which—although the focus may be on, for example, novices or specific actors in a mythic performance—concern every one of them, whether or not they are active participants. They are, one can say, fulfilling their Dreaming roles. Among the Aranda, especially, but also in other Desert areas, each person, male and female, is a reincarnated 'ancestral' spirit being: within him or her is an essential sacred essence. It is *that* which is believed to be within all persons, expressed in symbolic *tjurunga* form, and which in fact defines the sacredness of ritual.

3. Death

The northern Bidjandjara occasionally refer to a dead person as having 'sat down' (Munn 1970: 150), as having left behind something of himself. At death, the living must care for the deceased's country and its relics: yet the dead (in their spirit form, *guran*, equivalent to Desert *gordi*) are bound to that land.

The Aranda (Strehlow 1947: 42-6) draw a parallel between the 'totemic' spirit beings who 'turn into' *tjurunga*—who change their state, without changing their essential sacredness—and the dead who also, through their death, 'turn into' something else. In the former case, in becoming *tjurunga*, they are inevitably caught within the eternal, in contrast to their apparent mobility within the creative era when they travelled across the land. However, they, or part of them, may 'escape' by entering a female who comes close to their particular site. With contemporary man, the situation is not very different. Strehlow (*ibid.*: 43) states that 'death ends all', and he speaks of 'the final annihilation of the soul'. However, this is not clear-cut. He also says that a western Aranda person's soul goes to the Land of the Dead, where it is destroyed by Lightning: in other cases, it (they) may go to 'where their *tjurunga* bodies were resting'. It is this last point which fits in with Spencer and Gillen's (*ibid.*: 497-511) evidence. They say that a *tjurunga* may be buried with a man (*ibid.*: 498). Again, as in the delayed-mourning ritual of Urpmilchima, which is held in order to break various tabus associated with a widow, the deceased's spirit watches over the proceedings. The spirit may continue to serve as a guardian for her friends and relatives, see that no harm befalls them, and even visit them in dreams, etc. The cleared side of the grave faces the site from which the Dreaming spirit of the deceased came; and the spirit of the dead lives with his spirit double as a manifestation of that Dreaming being. (See also Spencer and Gillen 1904: 505-55.)

Although the information is sparse, it seems highly likely that, in spite of the annihilation theory (which can be interpreted as referring to the physical aspect of man), the basic underlying concept rests on the spiritual continuity of the deceased person, with its eventual mergence with a spirit double, that in turn is identified with a relevant Dreaming being who is responsible for its re-emergence.* As with the northern Bidjandjara, the 'dead' are

---

* Of particular importance in relation to the Aranda is Strehlow (1964b: 723-52). In this contribution, he provides additional material on birth and on death. At the time of writing this fascicle, I did not have access to this study. He mentions (*ibid.*: 731 *et seq.*) that 'At birth, every human being that

always present, in their spirit form, even if their individual human or personal names are lost. It is not the person as such who requires identification. Rather, it is his or her Dreaming spirit allocation, since this is considered to be the most significant aspect of man.

D. Religious Rituals: the Eastern Prong

In earlier literature, Spencer and Gillen (1904: 177-225, 226-55, 257-82, 283-319; 1938: 112-27, 128-66, 167-211) and C. Strehlow (1907-20) provide a fairly wide coverage of ritual life. Two relevant points, among many others, emerge from this. The first refers to rituals which women witness and in which they participate. The second is that the great majority of the rituals relate to episodes in the life and travels of 'totemic' spirit beings, and that these are of a secret-sacred character to which only initiated men are admitted. Some of these last may be classified as initiatory, since the process of admitting youths and men to their cult lodge rituals is a continuing one. However, not all of them are regarded in that way, and many are carried out without the induction of others. The outstanding Aranda rituals are the *intichiuma*; this is (apparently) a term which refers to 'totemic' rituals pertaining to increase (or maintenance of food supplies or natural species). Each local descent group has its own cycle or cycle-section (Spencer and Gillen 1938: 169). Spencer and Gillen describe those relevant to the Witchetty Grub, the Emu, Hakea Flower, Gumtree leaf manna, Honey Ant, and Water (and Kangaroo). Further Aranda examples are given in Spencer and Gillen (1904), along with descriptions of rituals associated with adjacent tribal groups. In all of these, actions and adventures of the mythic beings are dramatized, the actors being decorated with designs in feather-down and wearing or using a variety of ritual emblems: additionally, elaborate ground 'drawings' are made.

Probably a distinction can be drawn between the *intichiuma* on one hand and, on the other, rituals which do not necessarily emphasize increase and where the focus is more on the actions of the Dreaming beings themselves. Many of these myth-ritual cycles have a relatively wide currency. A case in point is the Mungamunga (Munga-munga), who arose near Tjinqurokera (close to Tennant Creek) in Waramunga country (Spencer and Gillen *ibid.*: 303-6). These Dreaming women are quite obviously associated with the northern Mungamunga-Gadjari cult (see Part Four): yam sticks left by them become trees; and the yams they dropped in the course of their travels become *tjurunga*. In the ritual associated with these mythic beings, men decorate themselves as the Mungamunga. Also, the 'Wollunqua' rituals of the Waramunga (Spencer and Gillen *ibid.*: 226-55) show close resemblance to the Jarapiri (Yarapiri; Mountford 1968). Wollunqua was a mythic snake, probably a Rainbow Snake, which lay hidden in a valley within the Murchison Range (south-east of Tennant Creek): from there it travelled westward. At various sites it stood upright searching for a place where it could go into and under the ground and so return to its home site, but only when it reached Ununtumurra was it able to do this. Associated rites re-

---

came into the world was no longer regarded merely as the offspring of human parents, but as a reborn part of a supernatural being. It was believed that anyone looking at a man or a woman could see before him the original totemic ancestor or ancestress'. Or, again (*ibid.*: 739 *et seq.*), that at death 'The second (and immortal) soul returned to the dead man's conception site whence it had first emerged in order to be incarnated in a human being: this immortal spark became reabsorbed into the "life" of the totemic ancestors, and was hence taken up once more by the eternal landscape'.

enact its wanderings. In one, men build up a long mound, tapering at each end, with a meandering band in feather-down and red-ochre representing the snake. The mound is finally destroyed by postulants attacking it with spears, boomerangs, clubs and throwers. This is followed by subincision, which in the case mentioned was carried out on three youths. In other rites, ground drawings are prepared. One especially interesting aspect mentioned by Spencer and Gillen (*ibid.*: 247) is that the closing Wollunqua was associated with the final mortuary rites of a woman of the Wollunqua totem.

Jarapiri is the name of a great snake which was associated initially with Winbaraku, near Mount Liebig in Ngalia (north 'Bidjandjara') territory. Other mythic characters too are connected with this site. Mountford's study (1968) traces the travels of Jarapiri and other beings, with a photographic coverage of the various sites they visited, and details their adventures. They went from Winbaraku northward toward and beyond Yuendumu (in Walbiri country). At one place, the young snakes carried the old one (their father) on their heads: he had been severely burnt at Urdurbul by the Wanbanbiri (the Wood-gull people) who had danced with blazing torches. In the rite associated with Narakabili, an actor is decorated with a curving line terminating on top of the headdress. An important site in this journey was Ngama, near Mount Eclipse, the temporary resting place of the Jarapiri party but also associated with other mythic beings. (See A. Capell 1952; M. Meggitt 1966: 110, footnote 202.) The cave painting at the Jukiuta cave at Ngama depicts Jarapiri and the Malatji dogs. The rites performed here illustrate the connections between Jarapiri and his party and other beings already linked with Ngama. Of especial importance are the Malatji and Latalpa snake women dances.

Mountford (1968: 11) mentions the fire dance which, he says, 'appears to dominate most of the present-day ceremonies of Jarapiri and his party'. He draws a parallel between it and a Waramunga fire dance held at Tennant's Creek in 1900 (Spencer and Gillen *ibid.*: 375-92). This has already been noted as a feature of intiation ritual. The Nathagura of the Waramunga differs in certain respects from the Aranda 'final initiation fire ceremony' (Spencer and Gillen 1938: 350, 365) which followed the Wollunqua. Women participate in it, and there is a mixture of license and restraint. Women dance before a special *wintari* pole. Men are shut up in a bough shelter and dancing takes place in front of it, while torches are prepared and placed against it. Women build their own hut not far from the *wintari*. Men rush toward them and the women seek refuge in the hut, while the men throw slabs of bark at it and dance, jeering before it. Much of the organization of activities in this respect is on the basis of moiety complementarity. The main section focuses on the throwing of long torches (the *wanmanmirri*). First, men paint themselves with red mud and pipe clay to prevent being burnt. When they are ready, they hit one another with these torches. Finally, lighted bark is thrown in the direction of the women and children, and the decorated men rush toward the *wintari* around which the women are standing. Spencer and Gillen (1904: 392) say that the sequence is designed to settle disputes. This aspect is taken up by Peterson (1970: 200-15), for the Walbiri. He locates three varieties of fire ritual: the *djariwanba*, equivalent to Spencer and Gillen's *thaduwan*; the *ngadjagula*, equivalent to Spencer and Gillen's *nathagura*—see above; and the *buluwandi*, which he discusses. The *djariwanba* is mythically associated with the Jarapiri (see above): and the *buluwandi* has its own myths relevant to the Stork (or Pelican) who lived at Inabaga. Peterson demonstrates a close structural connection between these three rituals and those described by

Spencer and Gillen: the torches used in the *buluwandi* are *wanbanbirri* (Spencer and Gillen's *wanmanmirri*).

One point emerging from the analysis of sacred material from the eastern prong of the Desert, is that it is basically similar to other Desert ritual. It is highly probable that Aranda data merge within that pattern and do not stand out as a-typical. Further, the linkages from south to north are clear, so that a common continuity in mytho-ritual themes is apparent. The emphasis on Aranda local group organization, with its focus on father-son mythic dramatization and identification, and on compartmentalization of local sites along specific mythic tracks, does undoubtedly suggest a different slant when compared with other Desert and Central Australian material.* But this difference is not at the level of content or of religious belief. However, Strehlow (1965: 131) speaks, as he does elsewhere, of the comparative lack of cultural conservatism in the Western Desert in contrast to the Aranda—among whom, he says, conservatism, in terms of ritual, myth and song, was intense: see also R. Berndt (1970: 10-11). And this is possibly an important factor, to be taken into account when placing the Aranda within the present scheme and classifying them as having a Desert culture. Meggitt (1966: 79-91) compares the Walbiri Gadjari with the Aranda *ingkura*. He notes differences between the spirit beings of the northern and central areas, and considers that those of the Aranda are more actually 'totems', 'more firmly integrated into the general totemic configuration than are the northern beings'. But this is only partly so, and in most cases where a mythic being has a 'totemic' referent it (he or she) is shape-changing. It is this characteristic which is important, and which emphasizes the humanization of natural species, etc. And this phenomenon is common to all Desert cultures.

The problem of ritual and mythic diffusion requires detailed consideration, if we are to categorize an Aboriginal religious typology. Here we can refer to it only briefly. Meggitt (1966: 85) notes Gadjari linkages with the Ngalia and Waramunga. The Mungamunga (see above) are a pertinent example (see C. Berndt 1950: 12, map; Meggitt *ibid.*: diagram 9), and there are others. Moreover, basic elements of ritual organization have a wide currency, even though there are variations. The mythology of Ayers Rock (Mountford 1965) provides us with a range, even though it is not detailed, which can easily be compared with versions relevant to the northern sectors of this eastern form, and with Aranda material. A bridge between Bidjandjara (or Andingari) and southern Aranda is to be seen in the rituals at Macumba (in 1944; noted above: see R. and C. Berndt 1945: 239-66).

THE ICONOGRAPHIC CONTEXT

a) *Tjurunga*

One outstanding feature for the whole of the Desert region, including its northern fringes, is the use of sacred boards of various kinds: farther north they still occur, but mostly in bullroarer form. (See R. and C. Berndt 1964/68: 366-72.) The boards go under a variety of names, but they have perhaps become known more generally by the Aranda term *tjurunga*. Spencer and Gillen (1938: 128-66; 1904: 257-82) have discussed these for

---

* Reference should be made to Strehlow (1964*b*: 723-52) and to his volume (1971*b*) which, unfortunately, had not been published at the time this fascicle was prepared.

the Aranda: but the best description is by Strehlow (1947: 84 *et seq.*; 1964*a*: 44-59). It could be said that the *tjurunga* 'industry' was developed much more highly among the Aranda than elsewhere in Aboriginal Australia, perhaps because of the concentration on the stone slab variety. The word *tjurunga*, however, covers a variety of meanings: both ceremony (ritual) and sacred object are called *tjurunga*, as are the stone and wooden-slab objects, bullroarers, ground paintings and earthmounds, ritual poles, headgear and sacred chants.

The *tjurunga* in relation to a person's conception, initiation and death, has already been referred to. In the years following a young man's initiation, he is introduced to rituals and *tjurunga* of his own and certain other cult lodges. When he is made an owner and guardian of the *tjurunga* of his own totem, he must undergo thumbnail removal. When the wound is healed, he is taken to the *tjurunga* storehouse (usually a cave) where the bundles of wooden *tjurunga* are untied and handled to the accompaniment of songs; the incisings are explained to him, and each person handling these presses them against his body. Then the party go to a cluster of stones and, removing the covering stone, reveal a red-ochred one beneath. A father leads his son toward it, and placing it in his hands tells him that it is his own body, 'from which you have been reborn' (Strehlow 1947: 116). Once a young man is in possession of his *tjurunga*, he makes offerings of meat to the old men, as he does too when he receives instruction in their relevant ritual and songs. The period between his being given his *tjurunga* and gaining full possession of all or most of the knowledge connected with it (or them) could be ten or more years. It is not possible to give even in summary the wide range of myths and ritual associated with the *tjurunga*. Strehlow (1933: 187-200; 1947) sets out a number of examples. In the Ankotarinja myth, for example, illustrations show this mythic being portrayed by a ritual actor 'wearing the *tjurunga* on his head with which he emerged from the ground at the moment of "birth"' (Strehlow 1933: 195 and plate 1). In another, Ankotarinja wears the great *tjurunga talkua* 'on his head, which fell from his head when his heart burned with anger against the *tjilpa* (Native Cat) men of Parr'Erultja [a northern Aranda totemic centre]'. Strehlow (1962: 2-7) also provides several photographs. depicting Aranda men at Hale River performing local totemic ritual, among the para-phernalia being a spectacular *tnatantja* pole and another emblem symbolizing the Milky Way. The *tnatantja* (called *nurtunja* by Spencer and Gillen 1938: e.g. 360-4, 627) is, in Aranda mythology, a powerful magical weapon, used by the spirit beings 'as a weapon or implement ... for cleaving great gaps in the rugged mountain ridges ...' (Strehlow *ibid.*: 23). Or, again, 'the *tnatantja* which had risen from the totemic ground "ever from the beginning", was ... "a living creature", capable of independent action' (*ibid.*: 24). The *tnatantja* 'is regarded ... as the greatest single instrument which has shaped the ... landscape into its present contours'. In this respect, as in others, these ritual objects closely parallel the *rangga* of north-eastern Arnhem Land.

b) *General*

The *tjurunga* 'culture' is intensified among the Aranda, but its influence spreads into other regions: the long *tjilbilba* board and bullroarer of the western prong of the Desert are expressions of this.

The rites surrounding birth and death, in so far as both Desert prongs are concerned, have few material objects associated with them. Almost the only exceptions are the western conical grave mound and the *njunjunba* mourning ring (which has its parallel in Bathurst and Melville Islands). In the eastern prong, birth and death are linked in general terms to the *tjurunga*. A child's *tjurunga* is determined through the mythic actions of an ancestor responsible for his conception; at death a *tjurunga* may be buried with a corpse, or, if not this, a spirit of the dead seeks the place where its *tjurunga* body rests.

Circumcision and subincision involve the use of bullroarers; *tjilbilba* are shown to novices after subincision in the western prong, and in the eastern prong thread-crosses (*wanigi*) are common. Among the Aranda, after a novice has been shown his own local group/clan rituals he receives a large bullroarer; in the *ingkura* every youth receives a new *tjurunga*, bearing his own totemic patterning, and at this time all the *tjurunga* relevant to the particular mythic sequence covered by an *ingkura* are exhibited, along with *tnatantja* and *kauaua* poles.

The whole Desert is marked by its specific totemic cult lodges (of local groups), which are responsible for their own rituals, including initiation sequences. Each is the custodian of particular mythic paths (Dreaming lines or tracks). This means that, although all hold in common certain symbolic representations or ritual objects—sacred boards or *tjurunga*, or (in the western prong) specific relics—there is a wide range of body decorations, distinctive headdresses and appendages, special sets for almost each mythic sequence. Religious rituals of the west bring in the *tjilbilba*, *laralara*, *wanigi* and bullroarers. And the incisings on the *tjilbilba*, along with their interpretations, differ according to their mythic path. The same is the case with the eastern *tjurunga* (wood or stone). The *intichiuma* and *wollunqua* include a large number of dramatic re-enactments and a variety of feather-down body decorations, along with different and mythically appropriate ritual emblems. There are, too, elaborate ground paintings, and in the *wollunqua* a mound superimposed with feather-down and red-ochred designs.

Throughout this region, a major emphasis is placed on the sacred site, and this is well brought out by Strehlow (1970: 95-7), among others. These sites represent the 'reality', or the tangible validation of the Dreaming, if this were indeed necessary. They are in fact more than this. They can be viewed as extensions of particular persons linked to local groups, as representing in essence their individual mythic personalities, seen as being indestructible. The *tjurunga*, in one form or another, are the medium through which this is maintained. They are both a symbol of this linkage and an expression of what can be called communication between man and the Dreaming, between man and the great mythic beings. Among the Aranda, the focus is intensely personal. Strehlow (1947: 139) makes this point: 'Private ownership of the sacred *tjurunga* is a necessary institution, since even the members of the same family commonly belong to different personal totems. This is the logical outcome of the official doctrine of the conception site ...' This is counterbalanced by 'the unifying ties represented by the allegiance claims of the *pmara kutata* and by membership obligations to the local *njinanga* section' (see Strehlow 1947: 140; 1970: 102).

In spatial terms, the Aranda concern is for the sacred site and for the local descent group. For most of the Western Desert—western and eastern prongs alike—space is organized in terms of sites along specific tracks; and however important a man's linkage is with his place of birth and with its mythic associations, this is subordinated fundamentally to his belonging to that mythic track in broader social perspective. Of course, mythic tracks are relevant in both cases—among the Aranda, as among other Desert groups: and the real differences lie in the structure and the organization of territorially-defined units.

Aboriginal women's participation in religious ritual has already been indicated. In Spencer and Gillen's works, mainly focusing on the Aranda but also including adjacent tribes, it would seem that this is far greater than is actually spelt out there. It is essentially complementary activity that is stressed; and although women do not assume an executive role as the men do on their secret-sacred ground, their part in religious matters is not to be underestimated. Possession of, but exclusion from, is the theme of Spencer and Gillen, Strehlow (1947) and Róheim (1933: 207-65): for example, ownership of *tjurunga*, by virtue of conception linkage. As Strehlow (*ibid.*: 94) notes, 'The *tjurunga*-slab or rock representing the deathless body of a woman is carefully and reverently tended by the men of her totemic clan, whereas the living person who is the actual reincarnated ancestor is often treated without any respect . . .'—she does not share in its ritual significance.

Without elaborating such points, there is evidence to suggest (see C. Berndt 1965) that the explanation lies in male-female interaction and in the complementary roles of the sexes, and not necessarily in a compartmentalization of mythic and ritual knowledge. Women cooperate with men far too frequently and consistently in all aspects of religious life for this to be categorized simply as customary or conventional behaviour, without having a deep significance for them, both intellectually and emotionally. In the context of myth, and in the performance of secret-sacred ritual by men, female mythic beings are of considerable importance. Strehlow (*ibid.*: 94) says that such female ancestors are '. . . awe-inspiring figures, who enjoyed unlimited freedom of decision and action . . . [They] used to carry about *tjurunga* and instituted sacred ceremonies . . .' And men re-enact in ritual performance their travels and adventures as they do those of male mythic beings, paying the same attention to them, and without prejudice to their sex.

BIBLIOGRAPHY

Basedow, H. 1925. *The Australian Aboriginal*: Preece, Adelaide.

Berndt, C. H. 1950. *Women's Changing Ceremonies in Northern Australia*: L'Homme, I, Hermann, Paris.

Berndt, C. H. 1965. Women and the "Secret Life". In *Aboriginal Man in Australia* (R. M. and C. H. Berndt, eds.).

Berndt, R. M. 1959. The Concept of 'The Tribe' in the Western Desert of Australia, *Oceania*, Vol. XXX, No. 2.

Berndt, R. M. 1965. Law and Order in Aboriginal Australia. In *Aboriginal Man in Australia* (R. M. and C. H. Berndt, eds.).

Berndt, R. M. 1970. Traditional Morality as Expressed through the medium of an Australian Aboriginal Religion. In *Australian Aboriginal Anthropology* (R. M. Berndt, ed.).

Berndt, R. M. 1972. The Walmadjeri-Gugadja. In *Hunters and Gatherers Today* (M. G. Bicchieri, ed.): Holt, Rinehart and Winston, New York.

Berndt, R. M. 1973. Mythic shapes of a Desert culture. Contribution to Professor Helmut Petri's *Festschrift*, Institut für Völkerkunde, Universität zu Köln.

Berndt, R. M. and C. H. Berndt. 1942-45. A Preliminary Report of Field Work in the Ooldea Region, Western South Australia, *Oceania*, Vol. XII, No. 4; Vol. XIII, Nos. 1-4; Vol. XIV, Nos. 1-4; Vol. XV, Nos. 1-3. (*Oceania Bound Offprint*, 1945.)

Berndt, R. M. and C. H. Berndt. 1945. An Initiation Ceremony at Macumba. *In* A Preliminary Report of Field Work in the Ooldea Region . . . *Oceania*, Vol. XV, No. 3.

Berndt, R. M. and C. H. Berndt. 1950. Aboriginal Art in Central-Western Northern Territory, *Meanjin*, Vol. 9, No. 3.

Berndt, R. M. and C. H. Berndt. 1964/68. The *World of the First Australians*: Ure Smith, Sydney.

Berndt, R. M. and T. Harvey Johnston. 1942. Death, Burial, and Associated Ritual at Ooldea, South Australia, *Oceania*, Vol. XII, No. 3.

Capell, A. 1952. The Walbiri through their own eyes, *Oceania*, Vol. XXIII, No. 2.

Craig, B. F. (Compiler). 1969. *Central Australian and Western Desert Regions: an Annotated Bibliography*: Bibliography Series, No. 5, Australian Aboriginal Studies, No. 31, Australian Institute of Aboriginal Studies, Canberra.

Elkin, A. P. 1934. Cult-Totemism and Mythology in Northern South Australia, *Oceania*, Vol. V, No. 2.

Elkin, A. P. 1938/64. *The Australian Aborigines*: Angus and Robertson, Sydney.

Gould, R. A. 1969. *Yiwara: Foragers of the Australian Desert*: Scribner's Sons, New York.

Meggitt, M. J. 1962. *Desert People*: Angus and Robertson, Sydney.

Meggitt, M. J. 1966. *Gadjari among the Walbiri Aborigines of Central Australia*: Oceania Monographs, No. 14, University of Sydney, Sydney.

Mountford, C. P. 1937. Aboriginal Crayon Drawings from the Warburton Ranges in Western Australia relating to the wanderings of the two Ancestral Beings, the Wati Kutjara, *Records of the South Australian Museum*, Vol. VI, No. 1.

Mountford, C. P. 1938. Aboriginal Crayon Drawings, III, *Transactions of the Royal Society of South Australia*, Vol. LII, No. 2.

Mountford, C. P. 1948. *Brown Men and Red Sand*: Robertson and Mullens, Melbourne.

Mountford, C. P. 1965. *Ayers Rock*: Angus and Robertson, Sydney.

Mountford, C. P. 1968. *Winbaraku and the Myth of Jarapiri*: Rigby, Adelaide.

Mountford, C. P. and R. Tonkinson. 1969. Carved and Engraved Human Figures from North Western Australia, *Anthropological Forum*, Vol. II, No. 3.

Munn, N. D. 1970. The Tranformation of Subjects into Objects in Walbiri and Pitjantjatjara Myth. In *Australian Aboriginal Anthropology* (R. M. Berndt, ed.).

Peterson, N. 1970. Buluwandi. A Central Australian Ceremony for the Resolution of Conflict. In *Australian Aboriginal Anthropology* (R. M. Berndt, ed.).

Petri, H. 1960. Summary of a talk entitled 'Anthropological research in the Kimberley Area of Western Australia', Anthropological Society of Western Australia: mimeographed.

Róheim, G. 1933. Women and their life in Central Australia, *Journal of the Royal Anthropological Institute*, Vol. 63.

Spencer, B. and F. J. Gillen. 1904. *The Northern Tribes of Central Australia*: Macmillan, London.

Spencer, B. and F. J. Gillen. 1938. *The Native Tribes of Central Australia*: Macmillan, London.

Strehlow, C. 1907-20. *Die Aranda-und-Loritja-Stämme in Zentral-Australien*: J. Baer, Frankfurt.

Strehlow, T. G. H. 1933. Ankotarinja, An Aranda Myth, *Oceania*, Vol. IV, No. 2.

Strehlow, T. G. H. 1947. *Aranda Traditions*: Melbourne University Press, Melbourne.

Strehlow, T. G. H. 1962. Aboriginal Australia: Languages and Literature, *Hemisphere*, Vol. 6, No. 8.

Strehlow, T. G. H. 1964a. The Art of Circle, Line, and Square. In *Australian Aboriginal Art* (R. M. Berndt, ed.): Ure Smith, Sydney.

Strehlow, T. G. H. 1964b. Personal Monototemism in a Polytotemic Community. In *Festschrift für Ad. E. Jensen*: Klaus Renner Verlag, München.

Strehlow, T. G. H. 1965. Culture, Social Structure, and Environment in Aboriginal Central Australia. In *Aboriginal Man in Australia* (R. M. and C. H. Berndt, eds.).

Strehlow, T. G. H. 1970. Geography and the Totemic Landscape in Central Australia: a functional study. In *Australian Aboriginal Anthropology* (R. M. Berndt, ed.).

Strehlow, T. G. H. 1971a. Australia. In *Historia Religionum* Handbook for the History of Religions (C. J. Bleeker and G. Widengren, eds.), Vol. II, Religions of the Present: E. J. Brill, Leiden.

Strehlow, T. G. H. 1971b. *Songs of Central Australia*: Angus and Robertson, Sydney.

Tindale, N. B. 1935. Initiation among the Pitjandjara natives of the Mann and Tonkinson Ranges in South Australia, *Oceania*, Vol. VI, No. 2.

Tindale, N. B. 1936. Legend of the Wati Kutjara, Warburton Range, Western Australia, *Oceania*, Vol. VII, No. 2.

Tindale, N. B. 1959. Totemic Beliefs in the Western Desert of Australia, Part 1. Women who became the Pleiades, *Records of the South Australian Museum*, Vol. XIII, No. 3.

Tonkinson, R. 1966. Social Structure and Acculturation of Aborigines in the Western Desert. M.A. thesis in Anthropology, University of Western Australia.

Tonkinson, R. 1970. Aboriginal Dream-spirit Beliefs in a Contact Situation: Jigalong, Western Australia. In *Australian Aboriginal Anthropology* (R. M. Berndt, ed.).

Tonkinson, R. 1972. Ngawajil: a Western Desert Aboriginal Rainmaking Ritual. Ph.D. thesis in Anthropology, University of British Columbia.

CHAPTER SIX

CONCLUSION

This study is both preliminary and introductory. Detailed analysis of ethnographic material for the whole of the Australian continent must be made before it is possible to see clearly identifiable patterns of religious belief and practice. Here it has been impossible to cover more than a fraction of existing data. Even these, however, are selective. General implications which do arise must, of necessity, be tentative.

RELIGIOUS PATTERNS

Recognizing that certain areas of the Australian continent have not been adequately covered, we can nevertheless distinguish four significant religious patterns. (See Map page 23).

The first turns on the adaptive and mobile fertility cults centralized in Arnhem Land. (See Chapter Four.) They have spread in a roughly fan-shaped arc across north and north-western Australia—weakening, however, in contact with the strong segmentary systems of the Western Desert and of the Centre. These northern cults are quite highly structured, providing a network of linkages over an immense area. In all cases, they emphasize the complementarity of male-female principles, even to the extent of underlining the female principle in myth. At the social organizational level, they muster the resources of local descent groups (or their equivalents, oriented in either matri-or patri-terms) providing, first, a 'tribal' religion and, secondly, the beginnings of a pan-Aboriginal religion. In this last respect, their framework connects a wide range of 'tribes' by supplying a common system of belief and a common rationale for religious action: on both scores, they are sufficiently flexible to take into account indigenous elements, and through a process of accretion these come to be regarded as necessary attributes of broader significance.

The second pattern is focused on the Desert. (See Chapter Five.) It is what can be called a segmentary religious complex. Within it we can identify two prongs, with similar but slightly variant forms. The complex is marked by a compartmentalization of mythic tracks which correlate with particular local descent groups, each responsible for a section of the total body of religious knowledge. This organization is in contrast to the first pattern, where the religion is not divided up in this way. In the eastern prong, formalization is more noticeable than in the western. In general, within each prong, the religious orientation is strongly patrilineal and is obviously responsive to two social organizational traits: (i) a greater emphasis than in the north on semi-nomadic movements; and (ii) dialect-variation. The Aranda, in the eastern prong, place a major value on father-son section pairs, but not significantly on dialect-variation, although they support the general pattern.

The third example comes, area-wise, from the greater part of New South Wales and Victoria and is focused on the classical *bora* complex. (See Chapter Two, Section 3.) A num-

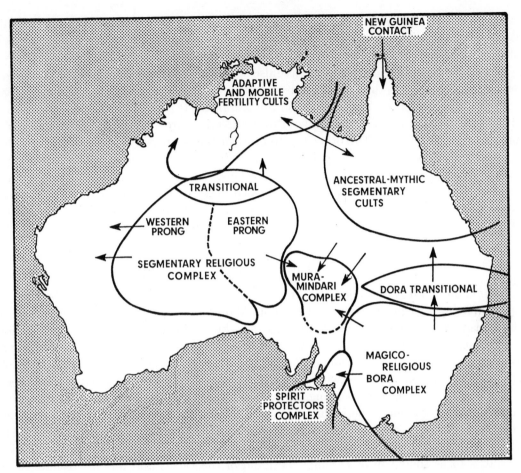

Religious Patterns

ber of characteristics lend a unique slant to this pattern. Two outstanding ones are: the degree to which 'magical' elements intrude on basic ritual, as expressed through the active participation of native doctors (or 'clever' men); and the appearance of *super*-natural beings who are conceived of as set apart from man. Within the context of both, a special relationship exists between man and the Sky World.

The fourth pattern requires further investigation. (See Chapter Three, Section 2.) However, tentatively, it can be seen as focusing on spirits of the dead who become ancestral and, in the process of transformation, are gradually merged with the mythic creatures which take 'totemic' form and are manifested at specific sites. These sites are the scene of increase ritual controlled by the clan in whose territory they are located. Cultic segmentation, although obvious in this area, differs from the Desert variety: ritual is compartmentalized, but intended to be relevant in broader social terms.

Such dominant patterns in Aboriginal religion are not, of course, all of a piece: they include variant and perhaps transitional forms. For example, to name only two, on one hand are those resulting from the impact of two differing systems, such as the Gadjari of the Walbiri or the *dingari* of the Gugadja-Mandjildjara. (See Chapter Four.) On the other hand, there is the *dora*. (See Chapter Three, Section 1.) Although information on this ritual system is slight, from the evidence available it appears to differ from the *bora*: magic in the *dora* is at a minimum, and competitive combat is an essential ingredient.

Two secondary-influenced patterns have also been discussed: and there are probably many others. One is located in the Lake Eyre basin, among tribes of roughly the Dieri type. (See Chapter Two, Section 1.) This focuses on the *muramura* beings and on the *mindari* ritual. Although external influences from at least three directions are discernible, a distinctive picture of this area remains. The other has to do with the Narinyeri confederacy of 'tribes'. (See Chapter Two, Section 2.) Again, these were influenced by upper River Murray and Darling River peoples with their Sky God traditions. However, religion in this area too has a characteristic flavour, perhaps best expressed through the spirit protectors and the extent to which females participated in religious ritual. There are also striking similarities with several aspects of Bathurst and Melville Islands religion.

THE LIFE CYCLE

Spirit children are, essentially, the intermediaries who bring life from out of the Dreaming, conferring this precious substance upon Aboriginal man as on all natural species. The Dreaming is the source of all life, and anything which touches it is by definition sacred. Sacredness is, therefore, a condition of living. But the ways in which this concept is translated into practice differ from one area to another. By avoiding a great deal of detail, a primary distinction can be drawn between the Arnhem Land view and that of the Desert. In Arnhem Land, generally speaking, life appears out of the Dreaming and returns there on death. What goes on in between, in physical life, has to do with tapping and manipulating that spiritual essence or power, channelling it in the direction of current and everyday affairs. Ritual is a simulation of *natural* sacredness. Immortality cannot be achieved in this life but is to be sought in or through the Land of the Dead: and for this to take place requires a socially concerted effort through the collective and delayed mortuary ritual sequences.

In the Desert approach, the situation is tackled differently. The assumption here is that the transition rite of physical death and its attendant mortuary procedures are not prerequisites to immortality. The conception-birth Dreaming (as spirit child), as in the case of the western prong, serves as an agent for a mythic being who desires to be reincarnated in a human person, and so influences a man's ritual participation as well as his local group membership. Within the eastern prong, this is more formalized. Living Aborigines are immortal, for within them reside the living mythic ancestors. In the mythic era, a sacred mythic being was possessed of the ability to 'change into something else'—that 'something else' varied, but the 'turning' also involved becoming a *tjurunga*. This meant that part of it, or one manifestation of it, escaped from its localized site to enter its human vehicle, a woman, for the purpose of re-birth: on the physical death of that vehicle it 'turned' once more. A spirit of the dead returns to where its deathless *tjurunga* body rests (at a specific site): the 'dead' are, therefore, *always* present—but the dead are always alive. A spiritual distinction is not drawn between the quick and the dead. The body is a physical receptacle —no more and much less so than the *tjurunga*, which is itself a symbol, a material symbol. A person is identified, not so much as a person, but rather as a mythic counterpart; it is that aspect alone which is eternal. The same thread of mythic identification is, of course, relevant for the Arnhem Land area, and in the Groote Eylandt example it is explicitly stated that the spirit of the dead not only goes to the Land of the Immortals—but returns with them to his own country.

Over the greater part, if not all, of the Australian continent the sacred, and particularly the secret-sacred, is (or was) categorized as something that is set apart—as dangerous, or potentially dangerous. To some extent this is implied in the association between spirit children and water and/or a Rainbow Snake, an association that extends, in the Desert, to spirits of the dead. The secret-sacred is hedged in with tabus and restrictions which bind to it, in varying degrees, certain categories of persons whether or not they actively partici- pate in it. Nevertheless, the evidence available suggests that although it is dangerous, it is a kind of danger which can, for those who are initiated, confer life and security. Or, viewed in another way, it is life outside the ritual ground which can be regarded as dangerous: within, all is secure—because, within, the sacred beings may be invoked and may intervene in the affairs of man, as part of themselves (or in their *own* interests). Ritual controls the dangerous and makes the unpredictable almost commonplace.

These same themes, in one form or another, are widespread. The Narinyeri variant emphasizes spiritual ratification, when a child receives a personal name which is linked directly to his patri-territory and to a specific 'totemic' protector. In the *bora* complex, the socially-unaffiliated or independent spirit of a child is seen on one hand as the vehicle for the matri-totem (as being symbolic of the flesh of man: or rather, the flesh of woman, manifested through Emu), and on the other as the receptacle for the assistant totem (underlining the spiritual-ritual associations of the father). Regarding the last, the assistant is seen as separate from man but something over which he has control. The mythic beings do not enter man at birth, although the independent spirit is from the Dreaming. On death, that spirit goes to the Sky World to join the immortals. In many respects, the Queensland (Yir-Yoront or Wik-Munkan) type is like a variant of the Desert situation. The clan totem resides in mythic spiritual form at the *auwa* site: spirit children emerge from it and after death return to it, become ancestors, and eventually merge with the mythic beings themselves. Variations on this theme do not weaken the contention that Aboriginal man in that area as in others viewed himself as being possessed of an essential quality which brought him close to being immortal, if not actually so in the flesh.

The intermediate period between the emergence of physical life and its disappearance on death is permeated by a concern for retaining or enhancing sacredness. In one sense, we can speak of all initiation as a re-introduction to the sacred. Although, in some regions, initia- tion is spoken of as a ritual death, it is in most cases thought of as being also a ritual re-birth: and this concept is especially conspicuous in the fertility cults. Initiation, then, is a re-emergence: a ritual re-introduction to mythic beings (northern) or a ritual enhance- ment of one's own mythic personality (Desert). Death is merely another form of initiation, and delayed mortuary rites (in the north as elsewhere) are really preoccupied with creating, or re-creating, life out of physical death.

Religious Ritual

Sacred ritual has many faces and is not by any means restricted to that which has been called the 'secret-sacred'. It is possible, and sometimes useful, to differentiate between

initiatory and other forms of ritual which do not have as their sole explicit aim the acceptance of novices: but both relate to sacred matters. Sacredness has really nothing to do
with the issue of who does or does not participate in any specific ritual action or sequence:
nor does it rest on the criterion of who takes a passive role and who a more active one.
Sacredness has to do with relationships between the material and immaterial elements of
man, between man and the mythic beings, and between man and the Dreaming. Initiation
rituals in Aboriginal Australia belong, indubitably, within that sphere. But they also point
directly and significantly to social problems. Every initiation ritual is a symbolic statement
about social relations and, especially, about relations between males and females. This is
brought out very clearly in the Wik-Munkan example, in connection with the significance
of bullroarers: these express sex relations and birth, family living and the continuity of
life (that is, through the production of human beings). Bullroarers symbolizing social
relationships are commonly used in initiation ritual, although cognate meanings may be
attached to them, and their specific uses differ. This is demonstrated too in Arnhem Land
rites of initiation, where male and female elements are seen as being both complementary
and, at times, in opposition. The contrast is framed also in other ways: for example, in the
physiological functions of the female as against the spiritual attributes of the male. (The
Dieri provide an example, among others.)

Not only initiation, but most other forms of religious ritual are focused, at least in part,
on problems arising from the economics of living. Since Aboriginal man lives in such a
close and intimate relationship with his natural environment and all within it, these *other*
rituals usually underline the fundamental significance of the Dreaming *vis-à-vis* those
problems. Man and nature are seen as one integrated, interdependent whole. Ritual ensures
that this essential harmony is maintained.

The great fertility cults of the north and north-western-central part of the continent are
designed to activate—through a combination of male and female elements—the natural
forces surrounding man. Life is a continuing process of birth and re-birth, decay and revival,
in nature, and in man. To ensure that this process is not jeopardized, spiritual intervention
is necessary. The *kulama* ritual of Bathurst and Melville Islands, although a-typical in
some respects for Aboriginal Australia generally, nevertheless emphasizes ritual control
over nature—in this case, through control over rain and floods, and prevention of sickness.
The same is true for the segmentary religious complex of the Desert. The Aranda,
although sometimes considered to contrast sharply with the Desert tribes, fit within this
pattern.

However, it is a mistake to over-stress the matter of economic expediency. Even where
maintenance of the natural species appears to be almost the only focus of such ritual, it is
also a highly symbolic frame of mythic reference embracing virtually the whole of socio-
cultural living, and not simply material survival. Probably the most direct emphasis on
life-sustaining and -producing ritual (that is, increase) is to be found in the *muramura*
rituals of the Dieri. There, even in initiation, a youth is given a bullroarer which is said to
aid in increase—but only under the inspiration of the *muramura*. The bullroarers of the
Wik-Munkan have much the same significance, but with wider implications. Again, in the
dora, the new names bestowed on initiates are believed to enable them to hunt more effect-
ively. The rites at the Wik-Munkan *auwa* are a further case of specific increase as a major
function of religion. Yet the complexity of religious ritual, particularly in northern and

Desert areas, provides a setting which, while certainly being economic in focus, has to do with a great deal more.

Virtually all Australian Aboriginal religious ritual emphasizes life. Mytho-ritual expressions affirm that the Dreaming is of contemporary relevance: the past, present and future are regarded as a continuing and uninterrupted stream. However, Aboriginal man has to deal with the present—even though that present is modelled on the past and the focus is on non-change. He must cope with the problems of living and with what we can call ordinary mundane matters. Both ordinary linear time and sacred, mythological or cyclical time are important to him and to his survival as a living person—irrespective of how the relationship between life and death is defined in his particular society. The *bora* is an extreme example. There, ritual was concerned mainly with achieving immortality, just as in Arnhem Land: but in the *bora* context, magical acts and dances underlined man's preoccupation with a hereafter. The initiatory and ritual grounds were constructed in such a way as to provide two symbolic 'worlds', connected by a pathway leading from one (the earth) to the other (the sky). At each ritual stage, magic of some kind was used in order to get in touch with the Sky Gods (Baiami-Daramulun). Although 'totemic' rites were held, ostensibly for 'increase' purposes, the focus was on achieving union with (for example) Baiami. Among the Narinyeri, the spirits of the dead passed, after cleansing themselves, to the Sky Home of Ngurunderi (as a major being). But the Narinyeri did not have the highly developed *bora* complex, nor the same kind of emphasis on life after death. In every case, moral and ethical considerations had no bearing on the fate of the soul. No sanctions were operative in this respect. The continuity of life after death, and a secure place in the Land of the Dead where such was recognized, were not affected by a person's conduct during his lifetime. Nor was rebirth, or reincarnation; and issues of status and rank—or of sex, for that matter—were irrelevant in this situation. And this reflects the basically egalitarian philosophy that underlay mundane as well as religious affairs throughout Aboriginal Australia.

Some divergences in Aboriginal religious patterns have already been discussed. Two points need further mention.

The first is the relative status of mythic beings and, in particular, of the so-called supreme beings. While earlier evidence is quite specific, it does not seem possible to speak of any mythic personages, like Ngurunderi, Baiami and Daramulun etc. as having ascendency over others. Usually such characters are seen in interaction with others and as part of an overall mythic network. Nevertheless, in almost all areas, except perhaps the Desert, one or more of them stand out from the others or are regarded as being dominant. The Djanggawul and Wawalag of eastern Arnhem Land, the Fertility Mother of western Arnhem Land, the Kunapipi, Gadjari of the northern areas, like the south-eastern Sky Gods, do receive attention exceeding that accorded to 'subsidiary' characters. Surely, one may legitimately ask, such beings are gods and goddesses in their own right?

Mythic beings were quite diverse, in their aims and interests, in the activities they pursued, and even in their physical appearance. Most of those mentioned immediately above, and others, were creative—they are viewed as being progenitors of present-day (human era) Aborigines; they shaped the environment, so that it became what it is today; they instituted or established and gave the 'law' to the people. Often they were *super*-natural deities in human guise, not necessarily identified with natural species or objects.

In some cases they are actually said to have been responsible for creating sacred 'totem' creatures, or causing them to be brought into being. But there were also non-creative beings and others in wholly or predominantly non-human form, for example in the shape of natural species or objects. And very many indeed, throughout the continent, were shape-changing: in the course of their wanderings they manifested themselves in different ways, at different times: some were transformed in outward appearance only at the end of their travels. Not least, there were tremendous numbers of secondary beings. All were sacred in some degree and all were of the Dreaming.

The second point is the relations between men and women. As a basic theme, this concentration runs through virtually all Aboriginal mythology, in regard to either content or context, or both. On the matter of content, female mythic characters appear probably at least as frequently as do those classified as male; in northern areas they are especially prominent, though not at the expense of their male counterparts. In strongly patrilineal Desert regions, male beings predominate. But even when they do, some proportion of myth and ritual takes up the question of male and female physiological functions. On the matter of context, women's knowledge of myth and their participation (actively and passively) in sacred ritual is much less circumscribed than has been recognized in the immediate past, while there is virtually equal participation of the sexes in Bathurst and Melville Islands in the contemporary scene and among the Narinyeri in the past. It is true that males do assert their authority on secret-sacred occasions. To balance this, in many regions (and particularly in the Desert), women have their own secret-sacred performances; and what they do have bears, at times, a striking similarity to what the men have. Nevertheless, men remain the main ritual custodians and repositories of sacred knowledge. Women's role is typically submissive, even where dominant aspects of female fertility are at stake.

Aboriginal religion everywhere on the Australian continent was oriented around two basic issues. One was physical survival, which was possible only through the power released by the mythic beings. The other was spiritual survival, and with this went a focus on the aesthetic expressions of man. The key to both was believed to rest in the Dreaming. Together, they pervaded all aspects of social living—not only mundane economic activities but also love-making and sexual attractiveness, dancing and song, the graphic and plastic and dramatic arts: all of these, along with other things, were cast in a sacred mould. Religion was a total way of life; and the transcendental was viewed as a necessary component, inseparable from living.

ILLUSTRATIONS

Preamble

With this Fascicle, we come to the important section on Central Australia. Our discussion falls into two parts, covering the western and eastern prongs of the Desert. Illustrations relating to the central-west of the Northern Territory are included here, because in that region are Aboriginal cultures which face the Desert and have been greatly influenced by it, so that much of their religious ritual closely parallels the 'central type'. At the same time, there are obvious northern influences, specifically in terms of the Fertility cult known more generally in this region as the Gadjari.

It has been necessary to exclude from our photographic series certain secret-sacred rites such as blood-letting and subincision. (See *Introduction* to these four fascicles, which appears in Fascicle One.) Western Desert Aborigines, particularly, are hyper-sensitive about this facet of their life: they are reacting against intensive European intrusion and afraid that their traditional religious ritual and sacred sites may be interfered with. I had hoped to include a series of older photographs originally taken by Sir Baldwin Spencer. Unfortunately, these are in the possession of the National Museum of Victoria and their publication was refused by the Director, Mr. J. McNally, on the basis of their secret-sacred nature. The fact that these photographs were taken well over fifty years ago; that a great deal of the ritual to which these referred has now been curtailed or abandoned; that a certain amount of it, while being sacred, was not secret, and that much of it has already been made available in varying publications—these points did not change the Director's decision in spite of the need to publish such material for scientific purposes. This means that our Aranda coverage is minimal. I should note that I did not approach Professor T. G. H. Strehlow for examples from his own large collection of Aranda photographic material, mainly because he has generously supplied these in the past in different contexts, and has his own publications in mind, and the secret-sacred issue is also relevant there.

The last part of this Fascicle is the concluding section, so that the illustrations for all four fascicles should be consulted.

Acknowledgements

Grateful acknowledgement is made to the following sources for help in supplying illustrations. Figures 11 and 12 come from Dr. Catherine H. Berndt; Figures 14 to 24 from Dr. Robert Tonkinson of the Department of Anthropology, University of Oregon, United States of America, who carried out his fieldwork when attached as a research worker to the Department of Anthropology, University of Western Australia. The Rev. A. G. Mathews of the United Aborigines Mission took the photographs shown in Figures 27 to 30. Figures 32 and 33 originally came from the Adelaide *Advertiser* and are marked as having been taken on the Mackay Expedition to Central Australia in 1926, of which H. Basedow was a member. These two photographs were probably taken by him. The expedition traversed the south-west corner of Central Australia, west of Mt. Olga, and went as far as the Petermann Ranges. Figure 32 is marked as being from the 'Pinto' tribe (that is, probably the Bindubi) and could have been taken in the vicinity of Blood's Range, as being the closest to that tribal area. Figure 33 has no tribal identification, but could be within the Mt. Olga-Ayers Rock area with Aranda affinities. (See 'Lifting the veil from the unknown: discoveries by Mackay Exploring Expedition', *The Mail*, Adelaide, September 18th. 1926, and 'Notes to accompany the Map of the Mackay Exploring Expedition in Central Australia, 1926', by H. Basedow, *Proceedings of the Royal Geographical Society*, South Australian Branch, Session 1927-28, Vol. XXIX.) Figures 34 to 35 also come from the Adelaide *Advertiser*. However, their original source has not been noted, except where the photographs were taken and the date (June 1935). Figures 36 to 56 have been generously supplied by Mr. C. P. Mountford of the South Australian Museum.

Some of the Figures illustrated here have been reproduced elsewhere in various other works. Figures 1 and 2 were illustrated in 'Aboriginal Art in Central Western Northern Territory', by R. M. and C. H. Berndt, *Meanjin*, Vol. 9, No. 3, 1950. Figure 25 is similar to one published in *The World of the First Australians*, by R. M. and C. H. Berndt, 1964/68, and three other photographs of the sacred site shown in Figure 26 can be seen in that volume (between pp. 176-7). Other photographs in the burial sequence shown in Figure 27 were published in 'Death, Burial, and Associated Ritual at Ooldea, South Australia', by R. M. Berndt and T. Harvey Johnston, *Oceania*, Vol. XII, No. 3, 1942. Figures 39, 40, 41 appear in C. P. Mountford's *Winbaraku and the myth of Jarapiri*, 1968; Figures 48-50, 53, 55-56 in his *Brown Men and Red Sand*, 1948; and Figure 43 in his *Ayers Rock*, 1965.

DESCRIPTION OF PLATES

Figures 1 to 10 belong to the 'transitional' cultural area.

Figure 1. A drawing in lumber crayons on brown paper from the central-western part of the Northern Territory. It depicts three dancers in the sacred Gadjari rituals (see Fascicle Three, Chapter Four continued, under Fertility Rites), dramatizing a species of green bird in its Dreaming form; they wear the elaborate *gumagu* headdress. The artist is Kalangga of the Njining tribe, although the ritual act is Walbiri; Birrundudu, 1944-45.

Photo: R. M. Berndt.

Figure 2. A drawing, in lumber crayons on brown paper, of a Rainbow Snake with a short mane moving through the sky, carrying on its back *maramara* native doctors who sit astride it. The Snake has arisen from Djabia waterhole, near Tanami, and is travelling to Galibinba waterhole, from which it heard another Rainbow Snake calling. However, when it reached there the other had disappeared. It then went on to Munggaduru well (left-hand side, bottom circle), where it remains. Below its body, between the two top waterholes, spreads an actual rainbow—its 'natural' manifestation. Native doctors are believed to have special power over such snakes. While the subject and waterholes are Walbiri, the artist. Lefthand, is Ngari: Birrundudu, 1944-45.

Photo: R. M. Berndt.

Figures 3 to 10 shows parts of the west-central Gadjari rituals, closely associated with the Kunapipi (see Fascicle Three, Chapter Four continued, under Fertility Rites); however, the separate enactments are more typical of the Desert cultures (of both the western and eastern prongs) than of the north.

Figure 3. A secret-sacred ritual ground, or 'ring place', in a creek bed at Wave Hill, west-central Northern Territory. Men are preparing for *gadjari* (Fertility Mother) rituals. The designs on their backs, in feather-down stuck on with blood, represent Lightning Dreaming. The central figure wears a *gumagu* headdress similar to those in Figure 1, on a basis of cane bound with human hair twine; its back is left plain. Singing proceeds while the men are being decorated; on the right, below a tin, is a pair of clapping-boomerangs.

Photo: R. M. Berndt, 1944-45.

Figure 4. Ritual dramatization of the mythic being, Djanba, in *gadjari* rites at Birrundu-du, west-central Northern Territory. See Fascicle Three, under additional sources. Men have spent several hours in decorating the participant, in feather-down stuck on with blood, His face is covered in the same way, and on his head the design is continued on a pad of hair twine fitted as a kind of cap. The actual rite takes a few minutes, in which Djanba moves forward holding the end of a spearthrower upright in front of him and then shakes himself. Behind him is the songman.

Photo: R. M. Berndt, 1944-45.

Figure 5. A ritual scene on the *gadjari* ground. The main figure is decorated to represent the Rain Dreaming: the vertical bands of the decoration signify falling rain. As in Figure 4, the actor is completely covered with feather-down from the waist upward, and the hairpad on top of his head bears the same design: he holds a pole over his left shoulder. Also as in Figure 4, the enactment consists of singing over a postulant to the accompaniment of clapping-boomerangs and body shaking.

Photo: R. M. Berndt, Birrundudu, 1944-45.

Figure 6. A *gadjari* rite on the secret-sacred ground in a creek bed at Wave Hill, west-central Northern Territory. Men stand round as invocations are called: three are clapping boomerangs. The invocations mark the conclusion of the ritual sequence, after the three decorated men (Cloud Dreaming) have completed their performance.

Photo: R. M. Berndt, 1944-45.

Figure 7. Men in the secret-sacred 'ring place' at Wave Hill, west-central Northern Territory. They are being decorated for *gadjari* rituals. One wears a *lalwada gumagu* representing the Lightning Snake. This headdress is constructed in a similar way to that noted in Figure 3: in this illustration the hair twine binding the emblem to the head is clearly visible. The main basis of this structure is a sacred board (*tjurunga* variety), covered with feather-down. On the left, the postulant with the vertical band decoration represents the Rain Dreaming (as in Figure 5), and the postulant below the man wearing the *gumagu* is also of the Lightning Snake Dreaming. As the decoration proceeds, relevant sections of the Gadjari cycle are sung.

Photo: R. M. Berndt, 1944-45.

Figure 8. A ritual scene at Birrundudu, west-central Northern Territory. The two postulants represent the Djundagal Snake Dreaming and are decorated with a distinctive design: the round dark circles on the chest and arms of the actors symbolize special balls made of bound grass which are used in a ritual ball game with mythic associations. The two men move down the cleared space, shuffling and rustling their bunches of green leaves.

Photo: R. M. Berndt, 1944-45.

Figure 9. A Lightning Snake, scene, part of a *gadjari* sequence at Wave Hill, west-central Northern Territory. The actor, decorated from the waist upward, wears a conical headdress topped with the *gumagu* emblem, which is a sacred board covered with feather-down. He postures, while men sing. In the foreground, on a wooden platter, is sacred bread (damper) which will be eaten sacramentally.

Photo: R. M. Berndt, 1944-45.

Figure 10. This is from the same ritual sequence as in Figure 9. Surrounded by postulants, and to the beat of clapping-boomerangs, the Lightning Snake Dreaming actor postures as the relevant songs are sung. The snake design extends from the actor's chest to the left side of his face, across and up the conical headdress on to the *gumagu* itself. Before him is a young novice witnessing the act for the first time.

Photo: R. M. Berndt, Wave Hill, 1944-45.

Figures 11 to 31 are from the western prong of the Desert.

Figure 11. Women at Balgo, southern Kimberleys, gathered on their ritual ground for *jawalju* dancing. See Fascicle Three. Their ochre body-designs symbolize a small Black Poison-snake, one of the mythic sponsors of this particular sequence.

Photo: C. H. Berndt, 1958.

Figure 12. Women on their ritual ground during singing in the *jawalju* series.

Photo: C. H. Berndt, Balgo, 1958.

Figure 13. Ritual headmen and postulants meditating over sacred *darugu* boards at Balgo in the southern Kimberleys. These boards vary considerably in size: all are incised with mythic, topographic designs.

Photo: R. M. Berndt, 1958.

Figures 14 to 24 are from Jigalong, near Lake Disappointment, in west-central Western Australia.

Figure 14. Men of Lizard (*djindjila*) Dreaming 'line', returning from their secret-sacred ground, encircle two groups of seated senior women who are arranged according to their generation levels: these women are the 'cooks' for the *mididi* sacred feast. See this Fascicle.

Photo: R. Tonkinson, Jigalong, 1963.

Figure 15. Ritually decorated men at Jigalong dance forward to meet southern visitors. They carry painted shields, and the man on the left wears a pearlshell pubic covering.

Photo: R. Tonkinson, Jigalong, 1969-70.

Figure 16. Decorated women participate in the welcome to visitors from the south arriving for a ritual sequence. They are sprayed with white clay, and three on the right carry green boughs for dancing.

Photo: R. Tonkinson, Jigalong, 1965.

Figure 17. Women at Jigalong, decorated and waiting for a ritual sequence to commence, welcome incoming southern people. They hold brush in their hands, for dancing.

Photo: R. Tonkinson, Jigalong, 1969-70.

Figure 18. Decorated and dancing women move behind men in their ritual welcome to the incoming visitors.

Photo: R. Tonkinson, Jigalong, 1965.

Figure 19. Women decorated in white clay for the ritual welcome.

Photo: R. Tonkinson, Jigalong, 1970.

Figure 20. While the *ngawajil* rain-making ritual is performed by initiated men on their secret-sacred ground, decorated children (as potential novices) await the men's return to the main camp: the designs are associated with the more elaborate ones of the men.

Photo: R. Tonkinson, Jigalong, 1963.

Figure 21. Men bearing rain-making designs which represent the Lightning Dreaming (*wiludjuru*). They are ready for the performance of the *ngawajil* ritual, and await the arrival of the southern visitors who will be introduced to (or initiated into) this sequence. The man in the centre wears a pearlshell incised with water designs and holds a bunch of feathers in his right hand; two men wear headbands, and each has a hair waistband. See this Fascicle. The *ngawajil* concerns the mythic being Djaramara.

Photo: R. Tonkinson, Jigalong, 1965.

Figure 22. Young men decorated with the *ngawajil* rain-making symbols await the commencement of the ritual. The designs refer to the Lightning Dreaming: they wear headbands and hair waistbands, and the central figure a pearlshell pubic covering.

Photo: R. Tonkinson, Jigalong, 1965.

Figure 23. A single actor in the Kangaroo (*malu*) Dreaming dance, on the secret-sacred ground. It is part of the Njungunj (*milgu*) 'line' (mytho-ritual cycle). The actor moves across the ground shaking bunches of leaves: he is decorated with a feather-down design and has a headdress of white and red ochred feather-down. The long shadows are from male onlookers.

Photo: R. Tonkinson, Jigalong, 1964.

Figure 24. Two actors representing the mythic being Moon. Each wears a beard (*njangi*), and holds a stick in one hand and a bunch of leaves in the other. This is part of the Kangaroo (*malu*) Dreaming cycle.

Photo: R. Tonkinson, Jigalong, 1965.

Figure 25. Exhibiting and meditating upon sacred ritual boards, which have been removed from a repository for this purpose.

Photo: R. M. Berndt, Giles, Rawlinson Ranges, 1959.

Figure 26. The gorge at Wonggarin, near Mt. Deering (Kathleen Range, east-central Western Australia). This site is sacred to the mythic being Njirana and the Gunggaranggara women (see this Fascicle). The sides of the gorge were cracked by Njirana's elongated penis, and horizontal marks and holes represent the *manimani* sticks used by the Gunggaranggara.

Photo: R. M. Berndt, Wonggarin, 1959.

Figure 27. Digging a grave for an Andingari man who died in 1939 at Ooldea, in south-western South Australia, on the fringe of the western prong of the Desert. The concentric circle design on the back of one of the men preparing the grave is of secret-sacred ritual intent, not associated with the actual burial: the man had attended the ritual (Wadi Gudara) but, in line with their normal practice, has left the decoration to wear off naturally. Those who dig and prepare the grave site are of the same generation level as the deceased.

Photo: A. G. Mathews, Ooldea, 1939.

Figure 28. A concluding ritual at first burial. Logs have been placed over the grave: women file around it, carrying bunches of leaves which are put on top. In the foreground is the conical mount symbolizing the mythic being Kula, the Moon man: an upright stick has been placed at its apex—this represents a yam stick, signifying that the deceased was a woman. See this Fascicle, Chapter Five, A, 3.

Photo: A. G. Mathews, Ooldea, 1939.

Figure 29. Men decorated for a ritual performance. Body designs concern the two mythic beings known as the Wadi Gudara. The four middle actors have *pindipindi* head ornaments made of whittled sticks with shavings at intervals.

Photo: A. G. Mathews, Ooldea, 1939.

Figure 30. Men decorated for the ritual sequence of the Wadi Malu (Kangaroo). They wear the small *wanigi* (thread-cross) headdress, while the large central *laralara wanigi* constructed on the basis of a spear is held by a local headman.

Photo: A. G. Mathews, Ooldea, 1939.

Figure 31. Two men in the mytho-ritual enactment of the Kangaroo (*malu*) and Dog (*baba*) at Ooldea. The actors move down the secret-sacred ground wearing the *wanigi* headdress constructed on a wreath of bound brush from which sticks protrude, each tipped with shavings: the human hair (or wool thread) is extended from one stick to another. The men carry bunches of leaves. Beside them, on the left, is a tall *laralara wanigi* stuck upright in the sand.

Photo: R. M. Berndt, Ooldea, 1941.

Figures 32 to 35 belong to the eastern prong of the Desert.

Figure 32. Ritual dramatization of the Wild Duck Dreaming by Bindubi (Pindubi) men. The headdresses, or emblems bound by hair twine to the head, resemble the *tnatantja* of the Aranda. The horizontal bound-bark extension, tipped with feathers, worn by the second actor from the left probably represents this bird's wings. The men hold spearthrowers behind their backs.

Photo: Mackay Expedition, 1926.

Figure 33. Ritual dramatization of the Carpet Snake Dreaming by Bindubi men. They are decorated with feather-down, and the two onlookers wear feather head decorations. Between the two actors is a small *tnatantja* pole, topped with feathers.

Photo: Mackay Expedition, 1926.

Figure 34. A group of ritual participants north of Tennant Creek, Central Australia, probably of the Waramunga tribe. The actual Dreaming is unidentified, but could possibly be associated with a secret-sacred section of the Wollunqua (see this Fascicle, Chapter Five, D. Religious Rituals: the Eastern Prong). Mounted on the men's conical headdresses is the Aranda variety of the *tjurunga mburka*. The first on the left and the second from the right have the tall *tnatantja*-like pole with horizontal 'arms' mounted on a long sacred board, with a meandering design in feather-down which continues down the conical headdress to the man's body and probably represent the Snake. The other men also have decorated sacred boards erected from their conical headdresses—except for the two men in the middle who are novices. All wear bunched leaves attached to their ankles for dancing.

Photo: Unidentified, but dated 1935.

Figure 35. A ritual actor, probably of the Waramunga tribe, north of Tennant Creek, Central Australia. Although the Dreaming this man represents is not identified, it is possibly a mythic Kangaroo. He sits on the secret-sacred ground after being decorated with a feather-down design. At the apex of his conical headdress is a sacred incised *tjurunga*, tipped with feathers.

Photo: Unidentified, 1935.

Figures 36-56 come from the C. P. Mountford collection of photographs. Figures 46, 48-50, 52-54 relate to the western prong of the Desert, Figures 36-45, 47, 51, 55-56 to the eastern prong.

Figure 36. Obtaining water at Erliwunjawunja in the Musgrave Ranges, south-west of Mt. Woodroffe: Bidjandjara-Janggundjara (Yanggundjara) territory. The young woman is decorated with sacred designs on her breast and arms.

Photo: C. P. Mountford, 1940.

Figure 37. At Erliwunjawunja waters, a typical permanent supply in the Desert. See Figure 36. This place has mythological associations.

Photo: C. P. Mountford, 1940.

Figure 38. The top background painting is of the mythic snake man Jarapiri (Yarapiri), associated with the fire ritual (see this Fascicle, Chapter Five, D. Religious Rituals: the Eastern Prong), in the Jukiuta cave at Ngama. Ngama was the temporary resting place of the Jaripiri party and the mythic home of the Wild Dogs (*maladji*). It is located just south of Mt. Eclipse, near Yuendumu, Northern Territory—eastern prong of the Desert, in Ngalia-Walbiri territory.

The Jarapiri's head is seen to the left, and the U-shaped designs surrounding the Snake are the camps of the Maladji. Beneath this, just outside the rock shelter, three men decorate a ritual performer with the Dreaming marks of Maladji. The rubbing stones for the ochres are beside him.

Photo: C. P. Mountford, Ngama, 1959.

Figure 39. The ritual performer shown in Figure 38, with four other men (three of whom have decorated him with the Maladji Dreaming). The man on the right is explaining the significance of the design that has been painted on a shield, said to be the same as that painted at Jukiuta, Ngama: that is, Jarapiri, and the camp sites of the Maladji wild dogs.

Photo: C. P. Mountford, Ngama, 1959.

Figure 40. Men re-touching the Jarapiri and Maladji paintings at Jukiuta cave, Ngama. See Figure 38.

Photo: C. P. Mountford, 1951.

Figure 41. Decorating a ritual actor at Ngama (see Figures 38-40) for the Jarapiri sequence. He is decorated with feather-down in the snake design which extends to his headdress, constructed of mulga twigs bound together with fur-string and covered with red plant-down. On top of the headdress is a white spiral representing one of the Latalpa snake women who accompanied the Jarapiri party from Winbaraku (Blanche Tower), near Mt. Liebig.

Photo: C. P. Mountford, Ngama, 1951.

Figure 42. Preparing a ground painting at Ulugiri, near Yuendumu in Ngalia-Walbiri territory. It represents emu tracks and the mythic Emu's sacred site, and will be used in ritual. Stones on which ochre is rubbed and mixed are alongside the artists.

Photo: C. P. Mountford, 1959 (but dated 1958).

Figure 43. Ritual performers at Ulugiri in the mythic Emu and chick scene: relevant to the Emu ground drawing shown in Figure 42. The two men are decorated in down; one holds the long *wanigi* made of human hair with an edging of down, tipped with emu feathers.

Photo: C. P. Mountford, 1959.

Figure 44. Three actors in a secret-sacred ritual. The reclining actor is Kangaroo; the other two are Euro. A Bidjandjara-Janggundjara performance at Ernabella, in the Musgrave Ranges.

Photo: C. P. Mountford, Ernabella, 1940.

Figure 45. The two Euro Dreaming actors shown in Figure 44 move toward Kangaroo: the finale of this section consists of placing hands on the Kangaroo actor.

Photo: C. P. Mountford, Ernabella, 1940.

Figure 46. This depicts the same ritual sequences as illustrated in Figures 44 and 45: it is part of the Kangaroo and Euro myth which also involves Djurdju (or *djulgi*), a night owl, and relates to circumcision and blood-letting. In this scene, a ritual performer is carrying out his act: he represents Djurdju and has a small thread-cross *wanigi* on his head. This performance took place at Niunja in the Mann Range, at Mt. Cockburn, in Central Australia.

Photo: C. P. Mountford, Mann Range, 1940.

Figure 47. A ritual performer representing the blind Wood Pigeon Dreaming: this sequence belongs to the Wild Turkey cycle. The bound bunch of feathers is tied to the top of his head. The blind mythic being Wood Pigeon in a state of extreme thirst gropes along the ground in search of water. At last he comes to a waterhole (dug on the ritual ground), Overjoyed, he splashes his face and drinks noisily and greedily. In the Figure, he is shown splashing his face, above the hole.

Photo: C. P. Mountford, Ernabella, 1940.

Figure 48. A group of singers in a circumcisional sequence. As they sing, they beat rhythmically on a sand mound with sticks. The man on the right is stained with blood from a blood-letting rite.

Photo: C. P. Mountford, Warburton Range, 1935.

Figure 49. A circumcisional novice watched over by his guardian.

Photo: C. P. Mountford, Warburton Range, 1935.

Figure 50. The mythic site of Ulturna, in one of the valleys west of Kanbi in the Mann Ranges. The mythic woman, Kutunga, collected wild tomatoes and made them into cakes, which she placed in the sun to dry. They cracked in the process of drying, and are represented today by such boulders.

Photo: C. P. Mountford, Mann Ranges, 1940

Figure 51. This shows two men retelling the mythic story relevant to this *tjurunga*, which is of the Aranda stone variety.

Photo: C. P. Mountford, Haasts Bluff, 1942.

Figure 52. Sacred incised boards have been removed from their repository. The two men are talking about their mythical associations. Such boards are typical of the western and eastern Desert. In this case they are called *gulbidji*, and come from Kanbi in the Mann Ranges.

Photo: C. P. Mountford, Mann Ranges, 1940.

Figure 53. The two men shown in Figure 52 press their heads against the *gulbidji* in order to absorb some of the 'power' inherent in them: this 'power' is called *guranida*, and is distinguished as a 'life essence' derived from the Dreaming.

Photo: C. P. Mountford, Mann Ranges, 1940.

Figure 54. Sacred boards removed from their repository at Mulara waterhole, north of Mt. Davies in the Tonkinson Range. The beautiful incisings on the *gulbidji* are clearly visible.

Photo: C. P. Mountford, Tonkinson Range, 1940.

Figure 55. A rock shelter at Ayers Rock (Uluru), in Central Australia. Mythologically it represents the wet weather shelter of the Dreaming Marsupial Moles (*itjaritjari*): the footmarks of these creatures are now light-coloured marks on the floor of the cave.

Photo: C. P. Mountford, Ayers Rock, 1940.

Figure 56. Painting on the wall of a rock shelter associated mythically with the Hare-wallabies (*mala*): this long cylindrical cave on the western side of Uluru (Ayers Rock) is associated with blood-letting. In the immediate past, Mala men ritually released blood from their arm veins so that it ran down this back wall: both subincision and circumcision were carried out in this cave.

Photo: C. P. Mountford, Ayers Rock, 1940.

PLATES AND MAP

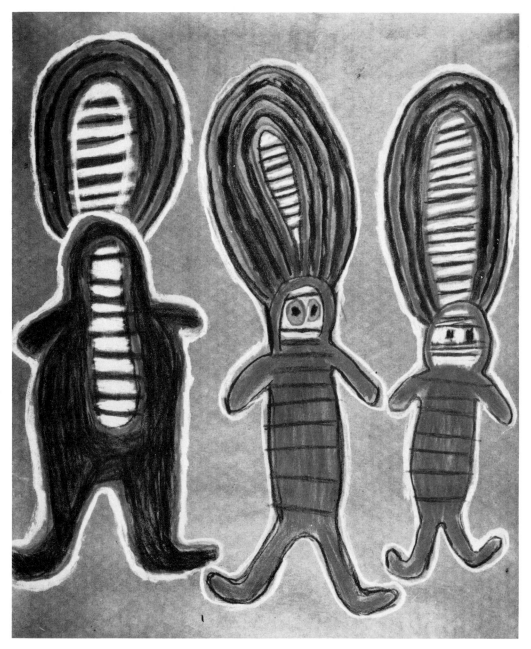

1. Drawing of three dancing men wearing *gumagu* in the Gadjari rituals, representing a species of green bird. Birrundudu, Northern Territory.

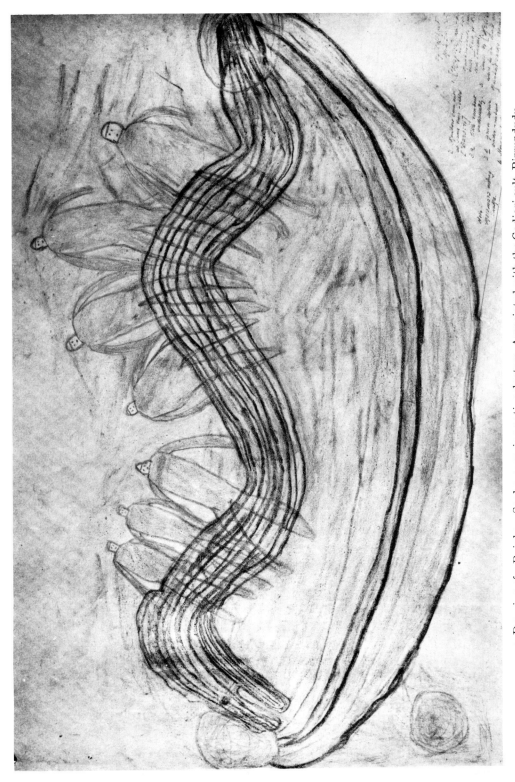

2. Drawing of a Rainbow Snake, carrying native doctors. Associated with the Gadjari cult. Birrundudu, Northern Territory.

3. West-central Gadjari cult. Men sing while being decorated for the rites. Wave Hill, Northern Territory.

5. West-central Gadjari cult. Postulant representing Rain Dreaming. Birrundudu, Northern Territory.

6. West-central Gadjari cult. Invocations being called after three postulants (Cloud Dreaming) have completed their performance. Wave Hill, Northern Territory.

4. West-central Gadjari cult. Ritual dramatization of the mythic being, Djanba. Birrundudu, Northern Territory.

8. West-central Gadjari cult. Two postulants represent the *Djundagal* Snake Dreaming. Birrundudu, Northern Territory.

7. West-central Gadjari cult. Men being decorated. One wears a *gumagu* representing a Lightning Snake; the two other decorated men are Rain Dreaming and Lightning Snake. Wave Hill, Northern Territory.

10. West-central Gadjari cult. The Lightning Snake actor postures as songs are sung. Wave Hill, Northern Territory.

9. West-central Gadjari cult. A Lightning Snake postulant wearing conical headdress topped with *gumagu*. Sacred food is piled on a wooden platter in the foreground. Wave Hill, Northern Territory.

11. Women at Balgo, Kimberleys, gathered for *jawalju* rites.

12. Women on their secluded ground during *jawalju* singing. Balgo, Kimberleys.

13. Meditating over sacred boards at Balgo, Kimberleys.

14. Dreaming Lizard men encircle two groups of woman who prepare the *mididi* sacred feast. Jigalong, Western Australia.

15. Ritually decorated men dance forward to meet visitors. Jigalong, Western Australia.

16. Decorated women participate in welcoming visitors to a ritual sequence.
Jigalong, Western Australia.

17. Decorated women await the commencement of ritual. Jigalong, Western Australia.

18. Women move behind men in their ritual welcome to visitors. Jigalong, Western Australia.

19. Women decorated in white clay for the ritual welcome. Jigalong, Western Australia.

20. Decorated children as potential novices for the *ngawajil* rain-making ritual. Jigalong, Western Australia.

21. Men bearing rain-making designs representing the Lightning Dreaming. Jigalong, Western Australia.

22. Men decorated with *ngawajil* rainmaking symbols. Jigalong, Western Australia.

23. An actor in the Kangaroo rite. Jigalong, Western Australia.

24. Two actors representing the mythic being, Moon. Jigalong, Western Australia.

25. Exhibiting and meditating upon sacred ritual boards. Rawlinson Ranges, west-central Australia.

26. A site sacred to the mythic beings Njirana and the Gunggaranggara women at Wonggarin, Kathleen Range, west-central Australia.

27. A burial rite at Ooldea, western South Australia.

28. A burial rite at Ooldea, western South Australia, showing the conical grave mound symbolizing the mythic Moon man.

29. Men decorated for the Wadi Gudara ritual. Ooldea, western South Australia.

30. Men decorated for the Wadi Malu ritual: they wear small *wanigi*, and one holds a large *laralara wanigi*. Ooldea, western South Australia.

31. Mytho-ritual dramatization of Kangaroo and Dog. The two actors wear *wanigi*-type headdresses and a tall *laralara wanigi* is stuck upright in the sand beside them. Ooldea, western South Australia.

32. Ritual dramatization of the **Wild Duck** Dreaming, by Bindubi men.

33. Ritual dramatization of the Carpet Snake Dreaming, by Bindubi men. Between the two actors is a small *tnatantja* pole.

34. Ritual performance by Waramunga men: possibly associated with the Wollunqua. Tennant Creek, Northern Territory.

35. Ritual performance by a Waramunga man: possibly of the mythic Kangaroo, wearing a *tjurunga* at the apex of his conical headdress. Tennant Creek, Northern Territory.

36. A young woman decorated with sacred designs, obtaining water. Musgrave Ranges, north-western South Australia.

37. A permanent watering place with mythological associations. Musgrave Ranges.

38. Three men decorate a ritual performer with the Wild Dog Dreaming design, just outside the rock shelter containing Jarapiri Snake painting. Ngama, near Yuendumu, Northern Territory.

39. Ritual performers at Ngama, near Yuendumu. The design on the painted shield, held by the Wild Dog Dreaming actor, is associated with Jarapiri, the Snake man.

40. Men re-touching the Jarapiri and Maladji (Wild Dog) paintings at Ngama, near Yuendumu.

41. Decorating a ritual actor at Ngama, near Yuendumu, for the Jarapiri series.

42. Preparing a ground painting of the mythic Emu, at Ulugiri, near Yuendumu.

43. Ritual performers at Ulugiri, near Yuendumu, in the mythic Emu and chick scene. One man holds a long *wanigi*.

44. Three actors in the Kangaroo and Euro mythic drama: the reclining actor is Kangaroo. Ernabella, north-western South Australia.

45. A scene in the mythic drama of Kangaroo and Euro. Ernabella.

46. A section of the Kangaroo, Euro and Night Owl drama. The actor represents Night Owl. Mann Range, north-western South Australia.

47. A ritual performer representing the blind Wood Pigeon, who finds water and drinks. Ernabella.

48. Singers in circumcisional sequence. Warburton Range, Western Australia.

49. A circumcision novice watched over by his guardian. Warburton Range.

50. The sacred site of Ulturna, representing wild tomato cakes made by a mythic woman, Kutunga. Mann Range.

51. Two men retelling the myth relevant to a stone *tjurunga*. Haasts Bluff, Central Australia.

52. Discussing the mythical associations of sacred boards removed from their repository. Mann Range.

53. Pressing heads against the sacred boards to absorb their power. Mann Range.

54. Sacred boards removed from their repository for meditation. Tonkinson Range, north-western South Australia.

55. A rock shelter at Ayers Rock, Central Australia, mythologically associated with Dreaming Marsupial Moles.

56. Painting on the wall of a rock shelter at Ayers Rock, Central Australia, representing the Dreaming Hare-wallabies.